What I Learned When I Was Ten

LESSONS THAT SHAPED
MY LIFE AND FAITH

J. ELLSWORTH KALAS

ABINGDON PRESS / Nashville

WHAT I LEARNED WHEN I WAS TEN

LESSONS THAT SHAPED MY LIFE AND FAITH

Library of Congress Cataloging-in-Publication Data

Kalas, J. Ellsworth, 1923-
   What I learned when I was ten : lessons that shaped my life and faith / J. Ellsworth Kalas.
   p. cm.
   ISBN 0-687-33592-2 (binding: pbk., adhesive perfect : alk. paper)
   1. Kalas, J. Ellsworth, 1923—Childhood and youth. 2. United Methodist Church (U.S.)—Clergy—Biography. I. Title.

   BX8495.K36A3 2006
   277.3'0823092—dc22
   [B]

                         2006013157

06 07 08 09 10 11 12 13 14 15—10 9 8 7 6 5 4 3 2 1
MANUFACTURED IN THE UNITED STATES OF AMERICA

What I Learned
When I Was Ten

This book is dedicated to
Angela
Lydia
Susanna

in the hope that through it they will
know more about their grandfather,
the world in which he grew up,
and the faith that has blessed
and guided his life

Contents

Foreword

WHEN WE REACH A certain age and place in life, most of us love to talk about the world in which we grew up. Before long most of us also learn that not many people love these stories as much as we do.

How is it then that I dare not only to tell some of these stories, but also to put them into a book?

Partly out of my belief in the importance of commonplace history; the kind of history that people otherwise put into novels. While presidents, kings, and dictators are finding their place in history books, the great mass of people are trying to make a living, find things to laugh about, loving when they can and worrying even though they know it doesn't help, and praying that God will see them through until tomorrow morning.

And more than that, I believe in the importance of eternal history. This kind of history is of course a faith-story. Either you buy it or you don't. But even those who don't buy it or who self-consciously mock it nevertheless can't escape it. Unless we deliberately expunge the idea from our minds, all of us sense that something in us keeps reaching to something beyond us.

In my experience, this eternal part of my story has made sense and value out of the rest of my story; and on the other hand, the rest of my story has provided not only the context for my faith story, it has also affected that story for both good and ill. If I were a more important person, I would perhaps call this book *Apologia pro Vita Sua*—the title of John Henry Newman's 1864 religious autobiography, and Latin for "A defence of one's life"; but even in my unimportance, that's what it is. It is the story of a very small chunk out of my now rather long life. I think that I thank God every day for the things that happened to me during those months from late 1932 to early 1934. And I cherish the simple, fond hope that perhaps some who read the story will find new purpose, gladness, and/or meaning for their own life journeys.

—J. Ellsworth Kalas

1

Winter of Wonder, Spring of Promise

I'M AN INSATIABLE READER, so of course I collect a good deal of unverifiable information. Much of it, I can't document later. When in the course of a day one passes happily and without discrimination through newspapers, billboards, philosophical journals, student papers, and maybe a chapter of a novel, one doesn't remember the source of each insight, whether treasured or trivial.

So I can't tell you where I read it, nor if the source was responsible, but I read somewhere that for most people the tenth year of life is the most important. It shapes, perhaps even controls, much of what follows. I suppose the reason this tidbit stayed with me is because it is true to my own experience. Can anything make a theory more surely true than that it has proved true in one's own experience? This is Newton's apple in every soul's search for gravity.

My tenth year was a long one. It began in August 1932, when I was still nine years old, and concluded in February 1934, just as I reached eleven. Everything that has happened to me in the more than sixty years since then is a product of those eighteen months. A psychiatrist would want to make a case for the influences of the oral and anal periods, and might want even to suggest the possibility of prenatal factors; if so, I would listen appreciatively. But it's that tenth year that picked up all the stuff from the days beyond conscious memory and conjured purpose from them.

Nor is it simply a matter of memory coming alive at that tenth juncture. I can reconstruct several scenes and dialogue from our visit to the Mayo Clinic when I was four years old. And I remember, early in my fourth year (I can date many memories by the houses in which we lived; this is an advantage of living in rental properties), sitting at the foot of the concrete steps of our yard, saying, "Good morning" to each person who walked by. This experience may have prepared me for the long decades of greeting people at church doors on several thousand Sunday mornings. I do wonder why that particular early childhood memory stays with me and how it is that, timid as I was, I dared so to approach each passerby. But with all of the earlier memories, there is nothing to compare with what I think of as my tenth year.

A Simpler World?

As we grow older, most of us insist that the world was simpler when we were young. It's an illusion, of course. The point is, we have hindsight to grasp the past, and hindsight is a great simplifier. It is possible, however, that the world was more accessible in those days. Not in the way that television, fax machines, and the Internet make things accessible now, but in the way intimacy makes life accessible. It was a world where automobiles had running boards, and where—though adults warned against it—you could jump onto the running board to ride a few blocks without asking your friends to let you inside. Soda fountains were accessible too; you could perch on a stool and sip a cherry Coke for a nickel, with the quality varying according to the skills of the soda jerk.

Politicians were accessible too. We didn't have their images on a television screen, but there was a good chance that even presidential candidates would get within driving distance (say, one hundred miles) on one of their whistle-stop trips, where you could see them up close and personal.

The year 1932 was an election year, and an exceedingly lively one. Herbert Hoover's run for reelection was being challenged by a patrician candidate (or so it seemed to us Iowans) from New York, Franklin Delano Roosevelt. We hung over the radio, enchanted by Mr. Roosevelt's patterns of speech, so different from our flat, Midwestern talk. But my father's heart was with President Hoover. After all, Mr. Hoover had been born in Iowa, and besides, Dad was an unrepentant Republican. Poor as we were in the Depression years that followed, Dad never believed that the Democratic Party was on his side. In human relationships, my father was the most democratic person I have ever known. I doubt that there was a prejudiced bone in his body. He needed no lessons in race relations. And although he was a Sunday school teacher and church officer, the prostitutes and small-time gamblers on his laundry route were to him nothing other than human beings who had made a wrong turn. They were, in the language of an old song, more to be pitied than censured. Indeed, I don't know that even *pity* would have occurred to my father, because pity implies judgment, even if kindly judgment. If he had known Robert Burns, he would have agreed with him, that "a Man's a Man [or a Woman's a Woman] for a' that." But when he voted (as he always did), he voted Republican.

Those were very dark days. When Iowa farmers couldn't get a fair price for their milk, they refused to sell to the dairies and drove caravans of trucks into town to pour their milk into the containers of us city dwellers, for free or for a donation. We were glad to fill our fruit jars and kettles with this very unpasteurized milk. Our fear of germs was subordinate to our shortage of money. There were instances of violence when some farmers decided to sell to the dairies, and bitter feelings ran deep among people who had been neighbors for generations.

Fear ran deep, too. I remember the evening Dad returned from work to tell us he had just learned that Frank had committed suicide the day before. "Hung himself in the barn. I guess he decided it was easier to die than to go through a sheriff's sale." I knew

Frank only from seeing him at family reunions—a slight man who looked better fitted to an accountant's office or to teaching medieval English than wrestling milk cans and plows. Now he was like a small side of beef, to be taken down and buried.

Nevertheless, we remembered how to laugh. There was the politician from the South, speaking on a national broadcast so that we got him in Iowa. "My opponent reminds me of the day old Davy Crockett thought he spotted a raccoon up in a tree. He took a shot, and it was still there. Tried again, and it hardly moved. It was only after the third try that Davy realized the raccoon was nothing more than a louse on his eyelash." My father and my brothers-in-law laughed loudly, but the women said, "That's such nonsense!"

If the radios gave immediacy to our news, the daily papers gave permanence. We waited for the delivery boy to throw our copy of *The Sioux City Tribune* in the vicinity of our porch. As a nine-year-old I looked each evening for the short front-page column by Will Rogers. Poor as we were in the years that began that October 1932, we never stopped getting the newspaper. We had no telephone, and our diet was modest by any standards, but we always had a newspaper. It cost only three cents a day and five cents on Sunday (even less by weekly subscription), but since my father—like many laboring men—earned only a dollar a day (six days a week), after losing his "good" job at the laundry, three cents was significant. Today's fifty-cent newspaper is, by comparison, a bit of a bargain.

At our house, and in the homes of our best friends and family, we had a vested interest in reading the newspaper. We believed that any day the news we discussed in private would become public headlines: the Drake Estate. As in Sir Francis Drake (1540?–1596), the first Englishman to sail around the world, favorite of Queen Elizabeth I, and the most famous sea captain of his day. For our family, and hundreds of others like us in Iowa, South Dakota, Nebraska, and Minnesota, he was the Moses who would lead us out of poverty and into wealth unimaginable.

Sir Francis Drake came to us by way of Oscar M. Hartzell; Oscar Merrill Hartzell, to be exact. For a long time, he was a man of mystery. We knew him for quite a time only by cablegrams sent to his trusted lieutenant somewhere in South Dakota or Nebraska, who then gave the word to other trusting souls for wider distribution. Our point of contact was Audie and Esther Sickels, at Esther's Barbershop, where Dad went for a shave every Saturday night. He did, that is, until he lost his job and had to resort to what we then called a safety razor. This was an appropriate name, by way of contrast with what had been the standard instrument before, the perilous straight-edged razor.

Audie was a wonderfully likable man who lived mainly by virtue of Esther's barbershop. Occasionally he cut a head of hair himself, but it always seemed beneath him. Not that he said so; it just seemed that he was made for more exotic things. Slight of build, with nicely graying hair, he cut quite a figure. He always wore spats in the winter. Spats, of course, kept out the Iowa cold, but they were also something of a fashion statement. My dad, for example, could never have brought them off. Fortunately, he knew it. Mother would say, from time to time, "Daddy, why don't you get some nice gray spats, like Audie's?" He would answer, "They're not for me." And he was right. Audie could have been the model for Meredith Willson's *Music Man*, except that he never found the right product. He had a remarkable collection of gadgets that he had tried to sell over the years. He was the kind of person who sought out the ads in the small-print section of salesmen's magazines ("SUCCESS IS POUNDING DOWN YOUR DOOR! THE WORLD IS WAITING FOR THIS PRODUCT! NOT A MOMENT TO WASTE!"). It was Audie's misfortune that he found it easier to be sold to than to sell.

And he was sold on the Drake Estate, no doubt about that. Each cablegram that got to him fourth- or fifth-hand was fodder for his portable typewriter. He'd type up the sacred message with numbers of carbon copies; the ones we received were usually dim enough that it was hard to make out the message, but we sought it out as carefully as a team of scholars studying the Dead Sea Scrolls. These were our irregular portions of manna, reassuring us that our investment in the Drake Estate was near fulfillment—yea, at the very door. Then it would be no time at all before we would

5

be filthy rich. Only, we didn't use the word *filthy;* rich was something so far removed from the world we knew that we wouldn't have thought of associating it with filth.

So let me tell you about the Drake Estate. There may still be time for you to get on board. Oscar Hartzell, who once ran for sheriff of Des Moines, Iowa, claimed to be heir to the estate of the first Queen Elizabeth's hero of the seas, Sir Francis Drake. We didn't know how Mr. Hartzell made this genealogical claim, but we never doubted it. He also reported that he had gotten hold of some sort of will, by which he was staking his claim.

The estate was said to be twelve blocks in the heart of the city of London that Queen Elizabeth had given to Drake out of her affection for him and her gratitude for what his conquests had meant to England. By the early 1930s, when Mr. Hartzell began his project, the property was estimated to be worth $22.5 billion. And that was long before the dot-com days, when no one knew what a billion dollars was.

But there was a problem. Mr. Hartzell had to prove in the courts that he was the rightful heir, and he needed money to wage this legal battle. That's why we folks in Iowa, Nebraska, and South Dakota were privileged to have such an historic opportunity. By investing in Mr. Hartzell's valiant effort, we could get a share of the proceeds. Oscar Hartzell made clear that his heart was dedicated to the common folks, so he sold shares in the Drake Estate at just one dollar each. At first he promised that the payoff would be at least a thousand dollars a share, but as time went by the promise of return went up.

We waited passionately for Audie's carbon copies of the Hartzell cablegrams. I still remember the cryptic message, "IT'S ALL OVER BUT THE SHOUTING." When Dad showed the tiny slip of paper to my brother-in-law Gene, he danced a little jig on the sidewalk in front of our house. My brother-in-law Tom was always more reserved; he simply shook his head in astonishment at the kind of money that would soon be his.

I think it was on the occasion of this particular message that my mother said, "Oh, Daddy, we ought to invest something more!" Dad smiled in the apologetic way that characterized him when all eyes were on him. "Well," he said, "when Audie and Esther showed me this message this afternoon, I went to the finance company and borrowed fifteen dollars [this was before he had lost his job, so fifteen dollars was a week's salary], and bought fifteen shares right away." Everybody in the room praised his foresight. No one suggested that it might be a foolish investment. How could you go wrong, at a thousand-to-one payoff, and probably more—and especially with the end so near that it was "all over but the shouting." In truth, that summer night we were shouting already, out there on the sidewalk.

Mother and Dad never lost faith in the Drake Estate, nor did Audie and Esther and hundreds of others. Oscar M. Hartzell was brought to trial in federal court for using the mails to defraud. The people in our little world were sure that Hartzell's trial was a result of big money interests and government corruption. Some weeks before the trial, while Mr. Hartzell was out on bond, he came to Sioux City to visit with some of his investors. My parents were among the privileged few who got to meet him. They were in awe. When they returned home that evening, they gave me a word-for-word report of the conversation. I remember Mother's special word of praise: "He's just as common as an old shoe." You might think this a derogatory statement. In truth, ordinary folk can pay no greater compliment than to say that someone of true distinction (like an heir to Sir Francis Drake) made no pretenses.

Hartzell was found guilty and went to prison for several years. Nearly twenty-five years later, reminiscing about those Depression years with my father, I referred to the Drake Estate as a hoax. I learned immediately that it wasn't a hoax in my father's eyes. By that time I had gone to college, to graduate school, and to theological seminary, and my father—almost always a soft-spoken man—nailed me with the strongest language I was likely to hear in our working-class home. "You're getting too smart for your own good," he said. This was very possibly a true judgment, but I don't think my attitude toward the Drake Estate was the best evidence.

Like everything else in our lives, the Drake Estate had to get some verification in the Bible. My parents, and most of the people with whom they associated, were simple, pious folk. In some ways I suspect they weren't that different from medieval Catholics in their attitude toward God and life. This is not to say that they were perfect in conduct, but only that their faith was a constant element in their lives. So when they got involved in the Drake Estate, they were delighted to find a reference (an exceedingly thin one!) in their King James Bible.

It was in the front of the Bible, in the eloquent dedication the translators wrote to their patron, King James: "For whereas it was the expectation of many, who wished not well to our *Sion,* that upon the setting of that bright *Occidental Star,* Queen *Elizabeth* of most happy memory, some thick and palpable clouds of darkness would so have overshadowed this Land, that men should have been in doubt which way they were to walk; and that it should hardly be known, who was to direct the unsettled State . . . " The translators' dedication goes on to praise God for sending them King James at such a perilous time, but that's not the point of my reporting. My parents and vast numbers of other earnest folks felt that the passing reference to Queen Elizabeth was evidence that the Bible was making reference to the Drake Estate. After all, wasn't it Queen Elizabeth who had sent Sir Francis Drake on his adventures? Nor did they distinguish between the Bible itself and the dedication written by the translators. It was in the Bible, and that was enough.

You can add this story to the thousands of other instances where people recklessly and sometimes artfully have used the Bible to suit their purposes. I suspect I've even seen such scriptural manipulation in sermons. I remember the afternoon the deaconess from our little Methodist Church stopped for a visit, and my mother took out our Bible to explain how the Drake Estate had a place in Holy Writ. It is much to that deaconess's credit that she gently avoided a showdown with my mother; the error wasn't likely to affect her salvation, and I doubt that the deaconess could have convinced my mother to see it another way. When one has so many dreams riding on a point of view, one won't give up that point of view without a fierce, angry struggle.

Tom Brokaw has named my generation—the generation of the Great Depression and World War II—as "the Greatest

Generation." Since I'm part of that time period, I fumble a bit on Brokaw's words, though I confess great admiration for the people with whom I grew up and set out into adult life. But if we were the Greatest Generation, our parents made us so. On the whole they were loving, but they expressed their love primarily through seeing that we had food on the table and shoes on our feet (though not in the summer; we went barefoot except on Sundays, to save our shoes), through their discipline, and through their unwavering belief in God and in honesty. They didn't often tell their children that they loved them; like Tevye's wife in *Fiddler on the Roof*, they thought their actions said all that needed to be said about love.

But they were as tough as the times. With fully one-fourth of America's basic providers out of work during the height of the Depression, I have no idea how they kept their sanity, let alone some vestige of hope. But of course I *do* have an idea; I shall talk about it in the chapter of this book entitled "A Child of the King."

My parents' generation had been raised to be tough. My father worked a six-day week all of his life. Only in the last few years of his working years did he get a week's paid vacation. My parents dreamed of owning their own home someday, but the dream didn't come true until they were in their late fifties. I will never stop marveling at their courage; not the courage of a moment in raw battle or in crisis, but the 24/7 courage to get up every morning, work thanklessly or struggle to find work, and eat modestly. (We had no nutritional pyramid of right eating.)

In the evening, there was respite. We went to church two nights a week and every night during revivals which, in our town, were fairly frequent. The other evenings, we sat and read the paper and listened to the radio—the Lux Radio Theater, the Little Theater Off Times Square (television is appropriately dull if you were raised on the imagination the radio evoked), and the comedians: George Burns and Gracie Allen, Eddie Cantor, Bob Hope, Jack Benny, and Ed Wynn, to say nothing of the genius Fred Allen. The radio brought so much magic and laughter in those days, that I become a bit sad when I see contemporary radio in its unimaginative and enfeebled state.

This is the world in which my tenth year, my year of decisions, was set. It is the reason I go back to my hometown, Sioux City, Iowa, almost every summer. I need to stop again at the schools where I learned, the churches where I worshiped, and the neighborhoods in which I grew up. Inevitably my two longest stops are across the street from the Lee Block, on lower Fourth Street, where we moved when the Depression hit our family, and a duplex on West Palmer Street, because it was at these addresses that my life was so largely shaped and given the directions that still are in force today.

I write about those days because the more our life stories move forward, the more they must also move backward. The more of my future I claim, the more of my past I reveal. And there I remember the insistence on simple virtues and the basic faith in God that shaped Brokaw's Greatest Generation.

Believe me, I know there were many shortcomings. We were insensitive to issues that our contemporary generation struggles to correct. Thus in our Monday morning singing assemblies at West Junior High School (an exercise that in itself showed a commitment to community and to simple beauty), we often sang, "My name is Solomon Levy, my store's on Salem Street," a popular folk song that was disrespectful of the Jewish people. I sang alongside my friend Sam Kaplan, not thinking the song might offend him; perhaps it was so much part of the culture that Sam took it in stride—but perhaps not. And of course it never occurred to us that the brightest girls in our class would ever be anything other than wives and homemakers, unless they became school-teachers, nurses, or typists. And we wondered a little while the Negroes (the best term we had then) in our school chose to tell the accomplishments of Jesse Owens when we gave our class speeches; weren't there other people to talk about?

On the other hand, I remember the sign I saw in the poorest hotel lobbies, where I helped my father pick up the laundry. We called them flophouses, but the sign on the lobby wall read "No loud or profane talking"—a sign that I think would profit several of the best establishments where I've stayed in recent years. And then there was the sign on the streetcars that I asked my mother to interpret for me: "No expectorating." It was a world where people sometimes spit, but they referred to the matter with a kind of pained gentility. Those in a contemporary generation who believe life's aim is to "let it all hang out," and who find their humor primarily in shock rather than in subtlety, will be amused by these restraints. I submit that this was the kind of influence that shaped the Greatest Generation.

I praise my hometown for a subtle form of education. They named so many of our grade schools after literary figures: Irving, Longfellow, Bryant, Bancroft. Such naming indicated that these persons were to be admired and emulated, and that they were altogether as important as the political, military, and financial figures whose names were on some other schools. It influenced even our schoolyard humor. "Jim's a poet. His feet show it. They're long fellows!" The humor was corny even for fourth-graders, but at least we knew enough about literature to get the joke.

This was the world of my tenth year. Everything about it was basic: Our food was unimaginably simple, our clothing so limited that some of our bedrooms had no closet; the only gadgets on our automobiles were those necessary for making the car run, especially the spark and the choke. And of course we lived very close to poverty and pain; our elders didn't try to shelter us from such realities. But we had a surprising sense of dignity and self-respect, and we believed that virtue had its own rewards, and we intended to pursue those virtues. Even in the least religious homes there was likely to be a wall-hanging with a scripture verse or a reminder of God: "Christ is the head of this house; the guest at every meal; the unseen listener to every conversation."

This was some of what made the Greatest Generation, the generation that would survive the Great Depression, throw itself into the battlefields of the Second World War and pay for it at home with the rationing of meat, sugar, gasoline, and tires, and with the buying of war bonds. We were tough, and generally kind. I take my hat off to the parents of the Greatest Generation, who made us so.

2

Born Again

THE IDEA OF RELIGIOUS experience has been part of the Christian faith from its beginning. Our Lord set the tone when he advised Nicodemus that he must be "born again." The most notable early convert, Saul of Tarsus, came to his decision in a dramatic encounter with God on the Road to Damascus. When the jailer at Philippi came trembling to Paul and Silas it was with the classic question of experience, "What must I do to be saved?" (Acts 16:30).

But the organizing and soliciting of religious experience seems to be rather much an American phenomenon. We are the nation of the altar call. Billy Sunday, the great evangelist of the first half of the twentieth century, gave a phrase to our language when he invited his crowds to "hit the sawdust trail." Billy Graham, who symbolized evangelism for the second half of the twentieth century, had just as sure a trademark if not as exotic a one: "I'm going to ask you to get up out of your seats." Perhaps it was the frontier heritage in America that made this kind of appeal so acceptable, or the individualism in America that made this kind of public, open decision so natural. One way or another, this type of public appeal and public decision characterizes American Protestantism.

I grew up seeing this as the norm. When I learned that there were otherwise good people (like Lutherans and Episcopalians) who became church members by attending confirmation classes, in my boyish mind, I also understood that they had chosen a rather dubious way; and that while their Christianity might be sincere, it was nevertheless second class at best. During the testimony services at our little Methodist church, Brother Allen often arose to make the same succinct witness: "I thank God for a know-so salvation." This was a declaration that he could remember the time and the place when he had become a Christian, and the experience that accompanied it.

This idea may have been overdone, but it has some things to commend it. Religious experience isn't everything; theologically, the important fact is not our experience but God's action of saving grace. But the experience makes the theology personal. The theoretical becomes not only practical but also intimate. Someone has pointed out that the hymns of Charles Wesley are notable for their use of the first-person singular; in this, they are much like the book of Psalms. Wesley's hymns did so because they came out of a period of intense emphasis on personal religious experience. People sang about what had happened to them. They could "remember the time, and tell you the place." Such an experience is no better than the person who comes gradually and almost imperceptibly to faith in Christ, but it is warming and reassuring in its own way.

This kind of experience was emphasized in the revival services of my youth. We expected not only that people would come to the altar in a public confession of faith but that some emotional content would be part of the event. And although in my boyhood this type of evangelism was carried primarily by some Pentecostal and holiness churches, the mainline denominations frequently joined in. When Uldine Utley, the blondely beautiful girl evangelist, came to Sioux City, nearly all the major Protestant churches supported her presence as a community-wide effort, with the services centered first in the First Methodist Church, then in Grace Methodist Church in Morningside.

So when my parents said one Sunday in late October or early November of 1933 that instead of attending the evening service at our own Methodist church we would be going to the Full Gospel Tabernacle to hear an evangelist named King, I was ready to go. I was particularly fascinated to hear that he played a musical saw ("Sounds almost like a violin," my mother said) as a musical special. I knew it would be an exciting evening—exciting, at least, as we defined excitement in 1933 Iowa.

What I didn't know is that it would be the decision night of my life. I had several religious experiences before that night and have had hundreds and hundreds since then, but this was the night from which I date my personal commitment to Christ—the night I was born again, redeemed, saved, transformed. Find as many verbs as you want and I will still want for an adequate expression of that landmark evening.

The evangelist did, indeed, play the saw, and I thought it was almost magic. Mrs. King played some other instruments, and both of them sang; evangelists were multi-talented in those days. Then Mr. King preached. The sermon was primarily a description of how bad the world had become. He spoke of murder and adultery, dishonesty and drunkenness. He talked about the immorality of the movies and predicted they would become still worse. If he were alive today, he would have the dubious satisfaction of seeing how prescient a prophet he was.

When I think back on that sermon, I can't see what it was that convicted me of my need of a Savior. Nothing in the sermon was calculated to appeal to a ten-year-old boy whose major measurable sins were the day he cheated a grocer out of two cents and the times he had smoked dry leaves with some other boys. In the years since then I have prepared with great thought and prayer evangelistic sermons that I thought would reach people at some level of both logic and emotion, but I don't know that my logic has ever been that effective. Jesus said of the new birth, "The wind blows where it chooses, and you hear the sound of it, but you do not know where it comes from or where it goes. So it is with everyone who is born of the Spirit" (John 3:8). There are no truer words in the Bible. The manner of God's dealings in our souls is mysterious, indeed, and any evangelist, theologian, psychologist, or village crank who tries to reduce it to a formula is either charlatan or fool.

As Mr. King finished his sermon that night and the congregation rose to sing, I felt what evangelists call "coming under conviction."

Specifically, I knew the sermon applied to me and that I should respond to the invitation. It was not the first time I had known this experience. A year or so before, in a revival service at our little Methodist church, I began to cry during the invitation hymn. I remember several adults hovered over me in an impromptu committee meeting, trying to decide if I knew enough to be saved or if it was just a childish emotional reaction. They opted for the latter. Again, I confess that we don't know the ways of the Holy Spirit, but perhaps my parents and their friends who made that decision were wise. At the least, it has all turned out well in the end.

I don't know what song or songs they sang that night. I'm quite sure they sang several. Altar calls at those revival services tended to be protracted. If the evangelist sensed that someone was on the verge of decision (or candidly, sometimes even if only hoping so), he or she asked the congregation to turn to another invitation hymn or to sing "just one more verse" of the hymn already before them. Billy Graham's revivals have their trademark invitation, the simple but strangely eloquent hymn by Charlotte Elliott, "Just as I Am, Without One Plea." We knew a wonderful variety in my boyhood. I think I can still sing most of them without the aid of a hymnal. "Let Jesus Come into Your Heart"; "Only Trust Him"; "Softly and Tenderly, Jesus Is Calling"; the metaphor varied as did the music, but the mood of eternal earnestness was always there. There was nothing trifling about those appeals. Some gave a feeling of finality, like one of my childhood favorites, "Is my name written there, / on that page white and fair? / In the book of Thy kingdom, / Is my name written there?" And of course no invitation hymn carried more insistence than the one by P. P. Bliss based upon the words of King Agrippa to the Apostle Paul, "Almost thou persuadest me to be a Christian" (Acts 26:28, KJV). The closing verse was unrelenting:

"Almost persuaded," harvest is past!
"Almost persuaded," doom comes at last!
"Almost" cannot avail; "Almost" is but to fail!
Sad, sad, that bitter wail—"Almost," but lost.

Our age, liking to think itself more sophisticated, finds such an appeal inordinately emotional. But if one begins (as I do) with a belief in the value of the human soul, and if one believes (as I do) that we humans are blessed with the infinite ability to make decisions, then the subject deserves emotion. I submit that it deserves at least as much emotion as the closing seconds of a basketball game during "March Madness," or that which envelops the singing of an artist (I use the word loosely) popular with one age group or another. I confess, perhaps with apology, that my tastes in poetry and literature are now such that I prefer more subtle figures of speech and more imaginative use of meter. Nevertheless, I have undying regard for those invitation hymns that shaped my childhood. They may have been inelegant, but they were not trivial. They may have lacked poetic excellence, but they were never short on earnestness and passion. I honor them, as I honor all the patient folk who sang them tirelessly while the evangelist pleaded for just one more soul. I have not, since my days as a teenage evangelist, had the heart to extend an invitation of any sort beyond the four verses of a hymn, but I'm glad they went farther than that on the night in the fall of 1933 when I was saved.

And I was saved, have no doubt about it. I wept abundantly for my sins. At this you may be amused, since you perhaps have a limited perception of sin. What did a ten-year-old boy know about sin? This, above all, that when the invitation was given and without any urging from anyone, I knew so well that I should go to the altar, yet I resisted with everything in me. Something in my young soul knew that if I went to the altar, I was voluntarily giving up the rights to my life. This, after all, is what it means to call Jesus "Lord"; because when one makes Christ his or her Lord, the inner throne has been abdicated to him. I don't think anyone had explained this to me, but this is the sort of thing one knows. It's the kind of knowledge that marks one as a human: the instinctive knowledge that recognizes that God has a prior claim on our lives.

So I resisted the call that evening. I stood crying, in all my ten-year-old rebellion. My mother pleaded with me, as did Philip Erkmann, a good and kindly grocer who also was ordained to preach but rarely had opportunity to do so. My father, strangely, didn't enter the persuasion team; I really don't know why, except that my father always found it easy to step back and let others take the lead. I went to the altar, a plain bench that circled the platform (our church architecture was Iowa-basic). I have no idea what I prayed, or what others prayed over me, except that I told God I was sorry, and that I wanted to be saved.

"Saved" has a jarring sound, doesn't it? It doesn't leave much room for our sense of nobility and for thinking well of ourselves. I find that we're now inclined to use words or phrases like "commitment" or "call to discipleship" for this act of decision. In truth, there's more involved here than simply a choice of synonyms. "Saved" suggests that I am in trouble and that unless God helps me, no one can imagine how things will work out, while "commitment" ("We invite you to make your commitment to Christ") allows one to approach God with a good measure of self-worth. One might almost say that "commitment" implies that God is in trouble, needing the kind of resources I will bring to the divine cause when I come. "Saved" may have been an overly harsh word, but for those of us who have estimated our potential for sin, it is an accurately descriptive word. As I look back on my life and consider some of the temptations that were not only powerful but terribly attractive, I'm grateful I was saved that night. I dread to think what otherwise I might have done with my life. Advertising always appealed to me. If I had followed that course, unsaved, I wonder what products and what ways of life I would have tried to sell to the world? Politics also appealed to me, all through high school. Unsaved, how would I have used the power of office?

But that night I was saved, and it made all the difference. Miss Olson, my kindly sixth-grade teacher, didn't know what had happened to me, but she told my parents some weeks later that I had changed dramatically. When I had transferred into Roosevelt School that fall, she had given me a brand new desk. I proceeded almost immediately to deface it by carving my initial. I was unpleasantly bright, inclined to show off in the classroom—perhaps all the more since I had so little prowess on the playground. Miss Olson told my parents she couldn't understand what had happened to me as the semester went along, but that she was very grateful.

I wish I could tell you that my conversion has ever after been so impressive in its evidence. In truth, I proved repeatedly that it isn't enough to be born again; one needs also to grow up. The figure of speech in the new birth is a telling one. In the spiritual realm as much as in the physical, birth is not an end in itself, but a beginning.

Unfortunately, sometime rather early in my Christian experience I got an unpleasant dose of self-righteousness. When I think back on some of those years, I am embarrassed beyond measure. Somehow I had many friends and was always being elected to school offices, but I can't understand why because I was so often obnoxious. Some of my "unsaved" friends were far more generous in spirit, more kind in conduct, more thoughtful toward others.

How could this be? A great many that are disaffected by religion have raised the same question. I think several matters are involved. For one, religious experience works with the raw material it's given. We all have to cope with our genetic pool. For some, it's a struggle with lust, for others a passion for possessions, for others a generally unpleasant disposition. Whatever, the salvation we need is related specifically to who we are. From a theological point of view, when we are saved, or born again, we receive not only forgiveness from God but also deliverance from sin. In real life, this deliverance from sin often proves more complicated in practice than the evangelists usually indicate. Not that they are to be blamed. Spiritually speaking, they are the obstetricians who preside at the new birth, not the pediatricians who watch over the growing health of the infant. But regardless of who is at fault, living out the Christian life is a bigger assignment than one anticipates in the wondrous hour of salvation. And the stuff with which God's Spirit works shows itself dramatically in the kind of persons we become in the months and years following conversion. When we testify to our salvation, we ought to give great glory to God, but confess with abject humility that God's glory would be greater if heaven were privileged to work with somewhat better material.

There's another problem, an ironical one. I think it is symbolized in a majestic line from Katharine Lee Bates' great patriotic hymn/prayer: "God shed his grace on thee, / And crown thy good with brotherhood." After we become good, we need to see our goodness crowned with some other virtues. Instead, unfortunately, we often seem inclined to crown our meager goodness with self-righteousness. We sit smugly in our corner where we can pull out some theological plum and announce, "What a good boy am I!"

But it happens so subtly. At first after our conversion we marvel at what God has wrought in our lives. We are almost astonished to find ourselves more kindly disposed toward everyone than we were before. E. Stanley Jones, who is often described as the greatest missionary of the twentieth century, said that on the night of his conversion he wanted to "put [his] arms around the world." I know the feeling. But as time goes by the wonder of the experience naturally becomes more commonplace, until in time we begin unconsciously to confuse our goodness with the goodness of God. We begin to see ourselves as morally superior to others. The energy we should invest in pursuing a deeper walk with God we spend instead in passing judgment on what we perceive to be lesser mortals.

I think often of the little girl who lived for a time in a very religious body. One night she concluded her bedtime prayer with the petition, "And Lord, make all the bad people good, and make all the good people *nice*." *Nice* ought to be the most natural of dispositions for someone who has experienced the grace of God, and who has taken Jesus Christ as Lord and example. But all of us have to admit with embarrassment that many church people aren't nice and that some are flat-out unpleasant. When I hear that many restaurant servers dread serving the Sunday after-church crowd because they tip poorly yet are especially demanding, I feel very sad. If conversion doesn't make us nicer to be around and much more considerate of other people, it is, indeed, a religion so heavenly minded as to be of no earthly use.

And yet, with all of the disappointment I feel in the way my religious experience turned for a time into paths of self-righteousness,

I would never deny the reality of what happened that autumn night to a seeking ten-year-old. I was, indeed, *born again.* I was now embarked on a new way of life. My course would sometimes be erratic. I would not always be a good example of the faith I claimed. I would sometimes fall flat.

But I would always get up again, and I would always keep walking toward the goal that was set before me that saving-night. Whatever my shortcomings, whatever my sins, whatever my fumbling days, I had found the course of my life. Now, more than seven decades later, I still look back on that night as the beginning of my new life. Everything since then has been shaped and directed by what happened that evening. I had been born again.

3

A Call Is for Those Who
Hear It

I HAVE SPENT MY LIFE in the Christian ministry because I feel *called.* You can judge from this that I believe in the concept of a call to ministry. In truth, this conviction has been a major factor in my life. But if anyone promises to tell you what a call is, doubt him. A good and simple man in my childhood said often that his walk with God was "better felt than tell't." I've lived with a call for a very long while—since I was ten years old, in fact—and I think that man's succinct statement applies not only to much of the Christian life in general, but for many of us, especially to our call to ministry.

Some people point to a dramatic, once-in-a-lifetime experience of call. I have no idea where my experience began. It was a settled matter, as I've indicated, when I was only ten; but I remember times as an eight-year-old when I arranged the six dining-room chairs in some sort of order so I could preach to them. They were unoccupied, of course, which is rather good preparation for any minister, fledgling or mature. Probably some would say that this little exercise meant no more than someone playing school or imagining as they throw a ball against a wall that they will someday be a big-league baseball player. Perhaps so. I might so dismiss it with a smile if I were now a banker or an advertising specialist. The point is that this idea of the Christian ministry is part of my earliest memories and that it is with me still today; yes, and that it is more dominant in my thinking now than it has ever been.

And I won't apologize for this prejudice I have regarding religious work or in my being uneasy with people choosing such work the same way they decide to be a chemist or a carpenter, on the basis of career testing. I say this even though I've seen a share of clergy who might have been sent in a more appropriate direction if only they had evaluated more carefully their talents and their personality. I understand the layperson who said of his pastor, "He says he's called, but I don't know where the voice came from, because I'm darned sure God wouldn't make a mistake like that."

Nevertheless, I'm sure human elements enter into the process of a call, career counselors or not. And I'm not uncomfortable with that fact. It seems to me that in all of God's workings in our world, great varieties of human factors are involved. It's generally felt that a disproportionate percentage of clergy come from small-town and rural communities, and I suppose it could be argued that this is so because young people growing up in such areas have fewer examples of professions than do suburban young people. We're often told that for several generations the best and brightest in the African-American community turned to the ministry because so few other positions of leadership were open to them. Facts or logic such as these don't diminish my faith in the reality of a divine call. I repeat, God works with the stuff of our lives and times. So while, on the one hand, Moses' call via a burning bush seems miraculous beyond doubt, it can also be said that if any kind of phenomenon were to break into Moses' life, it would likely be something in the world of nature since this was where he was living out his daily course.

In other words, I see many human factors in my own experience that cooperated with my sense of call. For one, I grew up in a churchgoing family. Every Sunday, morning and evening, and several nights during the week if there were revival services in town, the church was the dominant issue in our lives. I can still remember a particular Sunday morning when I was seven years old because, for some reason, we didn't go to church; this was so out of the ordinary that it has a singular place in my memory bank.

So, yes, the church was always a part of who I was, for as long as I can remember. But this is no sure road to the ministry. All of us know some adults who insist that they got so much of church when they were young that they want nothing to do with it now; frequent exposure alone is not enough to make a call. Indeed, since my parents were so much involved in church, and since they were not uncritical people, I learned while I was young that preachers are often the objects of unpleasant conversation. Logically, this could have spoiled me for the ministry; why would one want to enter a work that made one a weekly target of unpleasant comment?

Nor was my childhood church the kind that offered promise of glamour and prominence. In those days our family attended the Helping Hand Mission, a very plain and spare place on lower Fourth Street in Sioux City, Iowa. It had been started as a rescue mission by a man named George Search. There were services seven nights a week, and except for the preacher, the two deaconesses with their circumspect uniforms and perky bonnets, and a few faithful laypersons like my parents, the only ones attending were men off the street. There were a good many in those Depression years.

The Helping Hand had no pews, just wooden chairs linked in twos and threes. There were no stained glass windows, no altar ware, and no robes for the eight or ten people in the Sunday morning choir. Our pastor, Reginald D. Acheson, was a kind man, but always somewhat harried. This isn't surprising, since he had to preach a new sermon seven times a week and oversee the pathetic "Mission Hotel" that adjoined the church, a place where the homeless could get a bed for twenty-five or thirty cents a night. I repeat, there was nothing glamorous about this church experience, nothing to make me think the ministry was a profession.

On the other hand, there was glamour in the world of evangelism that played such a large role in my childhood. We tried to hear every visiting evangelist; and because Sioux City was somehow on many evangelistic circuits, we got a fascinating variety. I heard the one-and-only Billy Sunday during what proved to be the last grand sweep of his legendary career. I wrote him a letter as soon as I returned home that evening, explaining that I was going to be an evangelist someday (though I misspelled the word) and asking if he would send me the statistics from astrology that he had included in his sermon. He answered kindly in longhand, on the back of my letter, noting first that his data was from *astronomy*, not astrology, then signed the familiar "W. A. Sunday," a signature as famous in that day as that of any rock star might be in our day.

But I also heard speeches by dozens of lesser personalities, and I held them all in particular awe. I loved sports, and the early 1930s provided a boy with as large a sports pantheon as any single era in a century: Jack Dempsey in boxing, Big Bill Tilden in tennis, Bobby Jones in golf, and Red Grange in football. But for me, these persons were in the shade of any virtually unknown evangelist who came to our town.

My call includes a romantic element. My parents—probably typical of their generation—had a series of children in rather close succession; four daughters, as a matter of fact. Then, in the language of Scripture, mother "left off bearing"; and beyond the language of Scripture, she was glad of it. After eight years of freedom from pregnancy, however, she discovered to her distress that she was again with child. As she reported to me herself, she then cried for three months. I suspect this wasn't much of an exaggeration. Mother was a wonderful human being to whom I owe a very great deal beyond life itself, but she was capable of dramatizing life and of making herself the lead character in the drama.

As she reported to me soon after my conversion, she then told God that she would accept her state (not that there was much else she could do except make God continue to be uncomfortable with her crying), if God would let this child be a boy, and she would give him to the ministry. So that's who I am. Mother didn't bother herself with any scientific data that would insist that my sex was established before she had prayed; she knew only that in her distress she had bargained with God for a son and had gotten him.

Some years ago, a teenager who had heard this story asked me if my mother had told me about her experience before I felt my call to the ministry or after. I knew what the teenager was driving at, and I lied to her. I'm sorry I did, but I just didn't feel up to the theological discussion that would have been required if I had told the truth. The inference in her question was that my call was valid only if I had received it prior to this knowledge of my mother's experience; that if I knew of her prayer and promise, then my call was invalid because it was a product of my mother's story.

But I've come to look at it quite the other way. I think it is quite logical that it was this very knowledge of my mother's experience that the Spirit of God used as one of the factors that unfolded my call. If her story had not fit into a larger mosaic of divine leading, I'm very sure that in the almost inevitable teenage period, when we delight in rejecting the wisdom of our parents, I would have thrown out the call story along with all the other elements of outdatedness that young people attach to their parents. Her story was significant to me because it was consistent with what was happening in my own soul. And it was only one element in my sense of calling. It couldn't have stood alone, but it added to the call-awareness that was growing constantly in my soul.

It was an awareness that expressed itself in a very down-to-earth and practical way. I invested in a five-cent notebook (those were the days, you know!) in which I could record the best sermon illustrations and statistics that I gleaned from the sermons I heard. When I recall some of those illustrations, I think it merciful that I lost the notebook. I do, however, have a larger, three-ring notebook that I began only a year or two later. Its newspaper and periodical clippings would endear it, I think, to anyone interested in the mid-1930s and very early 1940s. Now and then I take it from the shelf and hold it, perhaps in the way a ballerina might clasp her first dancing shoes to her body.

People who have studied the nature of a holy call say that one of the valid elements is the affirmation of thoughtful people. If you're called, they say, others will recognize it. I think there's something to this theory, though my own case doesn't prove a lot. The churches we attended weren't overflowing with talented youth—or come to think of it, with youth of any kind—so when folks concluded that God's touch might be on me, it wasn't as if I were a North Star in a crowded constellation. Nevertheless, I'm grateful for those generous people and their kindly judgment, no matter what its limitations.

One evaluation is with me still. For a while in my mid-teen years, our neighbors across the street included a Negro couple (to use the term we used in those days). Ours was a very poor neighborhood, but nevertheless it was two or three blocks removed from a small racial-ethnic area, so these neighbors kept very much to themselves. But the woman of this family and my mother visited rather often on the sidewalk. One day the woman asked my mother if her son had a call to the ministry. Mother was taken by surprise, but answered yes. "I knew he was," the woman said. When my mother reported the conversation to me, I accepted it as a gift from God. I do so still.

But a call is for those who hear it, and sometimes those of us who hear don't listen as consistently as we should. During those years I was reading my Bible daily, completing the full journey through the Bible each year, and my basic moral conduct was scrupulous. But I remember the Sunday morning when Brother Morris (we didn't know the first names of most of the adults in the congregation; they were simply "Brother" or "Sister"), a rotund man of modest achievements, took my hand and said kindly but severely, "Brother Ellsworth, I don't believe you're walking as close to God as you once did." His words were true, and they stung. He helped keep my call in line.

That call controlled all elements of my life. When the junior-high-school principal told me I had been chosen to take Latin if I wanted to, I said yes, because I understood Latin would give me a better grasp of language and grammar, and I knew such knowledge would be important to my being a preacher. Our Christmas gifts were very modest, but when mother asked me for suggestions, I always knew of a book that I felt would help me "in my ministry." And while I was disappointed not to make the football or basketball teams in high school, it didn't matter as long as I was selected for the *a cappella* choir and for the Central High debate team, because these bodies would contribute to my calling.

But as much as I loved learning and realized its importance, my life took a strange turn during my senior year in high school. For years I had dreamed of the impossible, going to college, and now I was receiving college scholarship offers. Some good and kind people advised me, however, that if I went to college, I would become proud and God wouldn't be able to use me. So instead of going to college, I went to an unaccredited Bible school. As a result, I began my college career years later at age twenty-five rather than age seventeen.

The years between were by no means lost. I learned a great deal about the Bible and religious experience and the vast varieties of human creatures. And about myself. In case you wonder, I'm still learning more about all of these. There was a period during this time, however, when my parents feared I had lost my calling. I have before me a birthday card from that period. It's strange that of all the letters my mother and father wrote me, I have this one. It began, "Dearest Sonny Boy," and explained the presents I was receiving: a shirt mother hoped would fit, and a handkerchief she had made by hand, including the embroidered initial. Then, after "All Our Love," this painful word: "Wish we could rededicate your life for you for the Lord's work as we did the day you were born." I wish I could recall the hurt I caused my parents in those days. I am grateful beyond measure that they lived long enough to see my ministry come to substantial fruition.

My calling took a particular turn, thanks to my lifetime friend—Chris Zaffiras, as I knew him in the fifth grade and in high school, and Bill Travis as he became known when his career in radio broadcasting began to unfold. It was a Saturday in July 1946, part of the dark period that was causing my parents so much pain. I had fled to New York City as an interim refuge, knowing Bill would stand by me. He was showing me the city— Manhattan, to be exact—and on this day he had taken me to the Wall Street area. On a Saturday in July the area was completely forsaken, of course. But Bill wanted especially for me to see

Calvary Protestant Episcopal Church, where the great Samuel Shoemaker was the rector.

There, Bill delivered to me an extension of my call. "You think because of the way you were raised—the Helping Hand Mission and the Full Gospel Tabernacle and all that—that God is only interested in down-and-outers. God has equipped you to work with the up-and-outers. Lots of people can work with the down-and-outers, but very few can do what God wants you to do."

I still marvel at this speech. Bill was the son of Greek immigrants; I doubt that his parents knew more than a hundred words of English. We both were nurtured in poverty, in families where education was respected but belonged to another world. By the time Bill spoke his piece to me, he already had attained a good deal of success in his profession, as a news writer with ABC, but neither of us had a college education, and what we knew about a literate, middle-class or upper-middle-class world we knew only from our high-school teachers and from a few friends on Sioux City's "North Side." But Bill was as sure of what my ministry should someday be as if he were a prophet.

The dimensions of that ministry slowly, sometimes erratically, but always wonderfully unfolded: thirty-eight years as a United Methodist pastor (in Watertown/Concord, Green Bay, and Madison, Wisconsin, and in Cleveland, Ohio), then five years with the World Methodist Council, and since 1993 at Asbury Theological Seminary. I have realized many times that I am unworthy of the ministry of Christ, but I have never doubted the call. Which is to say, I have been caught between questioning God's wisdom and marveling at his grace.

As a boy, I saw myself as an evangelist, but I spent nearly forty years being a pastor. Along the way, however, I have held several hundred evangelistic missions, under a variety of titles: revival meetings, renewal weekends, spiritual-life missions—whatever the name, they have fulfilled my boyhood dream. And because I love learning and am in some ways more at home in books than anywhere, I have often been torn between two callings, preaching and teaching. By the generosity of God, I have been privileged to do both.

During my high-school fiftieth reunion, one of the finest and loveliest members of the class, Florence Ferner, asked me if I would like to see a copy of an interview that appeared in our junior-high-school paper when we were in the eighth grade. She mailed it a few days later. My answers in that eighth-grade interview were almost unbelievably inane. But when the interviewer asked what I hoped to be when I grew up, I answered something like this: "I want to be a preacher and to write books."

A call is for those who hear it. Its ways defy definition, and I suspect that in most cases—like mine—the call is refined, enlarged, made more specific and more general as the years go by. I know this for sure, that I am grateful beyond expression that God has entrusted me for these long-short years with a holy call. Thank you, Father.

4

Benito Mussolini and the Blue Eagle

I N THE WINTER OF 1933–34, the most popular symbol in America must have been the Blue Eagle. I can't prove this, of course, and I'm working from my memory of life in Sioux City, Iowa, which is not necessarily a representative sampling. But I suspect America as a whole was not, in this instance, too different from our town in the great, rural Midwest.

In spite of my father's vote, Franklin Delano Roosevelt was elected president in November 1932 and assumed office in March 1933. He moved quickly into a series of programs that were intended to bring an end to the economic depression. Today alphabetical abbreviations are a way of life; something that can't be put into an acronym is hardly worth noticing. But the idea was new in those days, so when the Roosevelt administration came up with programs that were popularly identified by their abbreviations—the AAA, CCC, NRA, FHA, TVA, WPA, and CWA, to name only a few—they soon were referred to by newspaper writers and by the general public as "the alphabet soup."

The greatest of these was the NRA, the National Recovery Administration, a code of practices for business and industry that set minimum wages and maximum hours and supported the workers' right to join unions. I think it can fairly be said that the NRA was the kingpin of the government's attack on the depressed economy, and although the Supreme Court declared it unconstitutional in 1935, while it lasted, it was, from a public relations point of view, spectacular. Tens of thousands of school children brought home beautiful pictures of the Blue Eagle, the symbol of the NRA, to post in their front window, to say that this was another home that supported the government's recovery effort. It wasn't until the Lyndon Johnson administration, nearly a generation later, that the "war on poverty" phrase was born, but the Blue Eagle in the window captured all the quality of a national crusade against economic evil.

So I brought home a Blue Eagle too, proud to be a patriot in this fight. But my mother wasn't sure. "I don't know that we should put it in our window," she said. "I've heard that it may be the mark of the beast."

People who have observed the extraordinary popularity of the *Left Behind* books and movies—and before that, the Hal Lindsey book *The Late Great Planet Earth*—may think the interest in biblical prophecy is a phenomenon of this generation. Far from it! From the vantage point of one who has lived through most of the twentieth century and into the twenty-first, the most surprising thing about the popularity of the books I've just mentioned is that they succeeded so well with so little going for them.

Yes, we have a full share of headlines these days, but for most of us, they're manageable. The 1930s were something else again. My earliest recollection dates to the spring of 1932. Someone who was then very popular in evangelistic circles—popular enough to rent Sioux City's public auditorium for a night—but whose name is no longer in my memory bank, agitated a large audience with information about the black shirts that were marching across Europe. I remember crunching into the back seat of our family car (a Durant, if I remember correctly) as we drove home from the rally, listening to my parents as they discussed the matter in properly hushed tones. I had no idea what the black shirts had to do with religion and the Second Coming of Christ, but I half expected those shirted hordes to occupy Sioux City before the week was out.

The years that followed, from my pre-teens to teenager, were good ones for those who wanted to read the Bible through current news headlines, because the headlines surely provided an abundance of material. Armies were marching here and there around the world, and dictators strutted their stuff with what now, after their demise, seems like amusing arrogance. That may be a significant fact in itself. In the Far East—a place on the globe that at that time seemed almost as distant as Mars—Japan was making itself heard. In Germany a frustrated artist, Adolf Hitler, built up his following so that by January 30, 1933, he was named chancellor of his nation, and a few months later made himself dictator. In Russia, Joseph Stalin had come to power in 1924, but in the popular mind Russia (or the Soviet Union) was not a power one mentioned in the same breath with Germany, France, and England; so for a time neither his growing power nor his atrocities got the attention Hitler's did.

And then there was Benito Mussolini. Modern encyclopedias give him minor lineage compared with Hitler and Stalin; but for many evangelists and amateur students of biblical prophecy, he was far more significant. He became Italy's dictator in the 1920s. In 1935–36, his troops invaded a helpless Ethiopia. At no point was he a really major player on the military scene, and he died in complete humiliation. But for much of the 1930s a certain type of Bible student saw him as the fulfillment of the prophecies of the Old Testament Book of Daniel, chapter two, and of certain passages in the Book of Revelation. Mussolini's prominence came as the one who might restore the Roman Empire, from which, these students said, the anti-Christ would come.

I remember when Dr. Charles S. Price came to our town. He had been a prominent Congregational minister and Chautauqua Circuit lecturer, who was by that time a Pentecostal evangelist. His book suggesting that Mussolini might himself be the anti-Christ seemed very persuasive, particularly since Dr. Price was an eloquent man, clearly several cuts above our usual visiting evangelists. We teenagers talked outside the summer tabernacle each evening, evaluating his sermons with our profound sixteen-year-old wisdom.

"He's no dummy," someone in the circle would say, and the rest of us would nod in self-complimenting assent.

In truth, circumstances were tailor-made for apocalyptic preaching and believing. The times were hard. When a high-school graduating class somewhere chose as its motto "WPA [a government relief program], here we come," numbers of other graduating classes picked up the theme. By 1939, there was a generation of teenagers and even some young adults who had no memory of economic security; their whole experience had been financial depression or the threat of depression. And despite all of President Roosevelt's creative and far-ranging programs, the economy seemed mostly to cough and sputter.

The only way out seemed to be an apocalyptic one, a spectacular divine intervention, the return of Jesus. If the congregation sang of "some golden daybreak" when Jesus would come, it was easy to get into the mood. Teenagers may have been more ready to talk about teachers or dates, but they got the overflow of their elders' tears and prayers. Their parents found it easy to pray with all sincerity for the Lord to come, and even the young sang with earnestness, "He's coming soon; / with joy we welcome His returning."

It's very easy to evaluate that generation with a condescending smile, and to find psychological explanations for their passion for the return of Christ. It's amusing, I suspect, to recall their fear that the Blue Eagle might be the mark of the beast; and a little later in that decade, the even-greater fear that Social Security was a sure fulfillment. After all, folk said around coffee and cake on autumn evenings, "If you can't get a job without taking a number, it won't be long until you won't be able to buy or sell without it, just like it says in Revelation 13."

It's probably true that when people said they were longing to see Jesus, their longing was one part faith and another part economic despair. I can't really think badly of them for that. In truth, I suppose that every generation since the first-century Thessalonians has in some measure longed for heaven in order to endure some struggle of earth. Only the rarest of saints in the rarest of moments wants God for God's sake alone. I think God, knowing that we are dust, understands that our love is almost always tinged with some unlovely characteristics.

As I have said elsewhere, the saints I knew in those days were a hardy lot. I would put them against any I've seen in the twenty-first century. They wouldn't compare with Christian martyrs in the Sudan, or some of the most courageous in the Republic of China, but they were made of the same stuff. They survived slogging poverty, jobs—when they had one—with no future, and a generally bleak world that held little if any discernible promise. But they kept singing. Years later I would hear a philosophy professor label them as the kind of folk who lived for pie-in-the-sky-when-you-die-by-and-by. But that professor never met these folk. They were tough at the core of their being. And I would contend that part of what produced that toughness were those sermons about prophecy.

In a peculiar way, those sermons also stretched the otherwise modest intellectual boundaries of many of the people I knew. They read their newspapers. The people in my poor neighborhood who went to church were much more interested in Germany, Italy, and the USSR than were those around us. I remember how I quite astonished my junior-high-school teacher with my knowledge of the Balfour Declaration, something I had heard about through a series of passing evangelists who saw in that document evidence of fulfilled prophecy. Of course those teachers also heard several inane things from me as a result of some of this same preaching, but any eighth-grade teacher (or for that matter, any college professor) who isn't ready for an inane insight now and then is hardly worth hiring.

The sermons were quite wrong, of course, in their conclusion. They intended to prove the nearness of the return of Christ, and as my colleague Dr. Ben Witherington has said, all of the predictions thus far regarding Christ's return have one thing in common: a 100 percent failure rate. The longer and the more carefully I read my Bible, the more I wonder how those evangelists of my childhood (and their contemporary successors) could ignore what Jesus said about his return: "But about that day or hour no one knows, neither the angels in heaven, nor the Son, but only the

Father. Beware, keep alert; for you do not know when the time will come" (Mark 13:32-33).

The point could hardly be clearer: We just don't know when Christ will return, and God doesn't really intend for us to know. Only one thing matters for sure. Again, in the words of Jesus: "Therefore, keep awake—for you do not know when the master of the house will come, in the evening, or at midnight, or at cock-crow, or at dawn, or else he may find you asleep when he comes suddenly. And what I say to you I say to all: Keep awake" (Mark 13:35-37).

That seems pretty clear, so one wonders why preachers and teachers and authors keep trying in the face of it to set dates for Christ's return. Some say, only half humorously, that while no one knows the day or the hour, they can know the season, so to speak. And in truth, there are numbers of passages in the New Testament that describe the kind of world into which Christ will return, so that a preacher can hardly resist noting similarities with the times in which he or she currently lives. It's interesting that scores of generations over the centuries have seen *their* generation described in those passages in the Gospels and the epistles.

The fact that generations have seen such similarities may indicate, on the one hand, the kind of egocentrism in all of us that makes us think our generation is special; thus, these passages must be describing us. On the other hand, it may be even more the case that the biblical descriptions of "the last days" are so typical of all the times in which we live that people have reason to say, "Where is the promise of his coming? For ever since our ancestors died, all things continue as they were from the beginning of creation!" (2 Peter 3:4). If in a peculiar way the best delineation of the last days is that they are rather much like all other days— "eating and drinking, marrying and giving in marriage" (Matthew 24:38)—then it is no wonder that our Lord warned that we might be unready. No wonder then that Jesus would say, "Keep awake therefore, for you do not know on what day your Lord is coming" (Matthew 24:42). We're supposed to be ready at all times, and a kind of preaching that urges simply being ready when one thinks the "signs are right" is in a very real sense a contradiction of what our Lord desired. We're to live always as if the Lord might come before the day is out.

In a peculiar way, I think the preaching I heard from those evangelists and pastors in my boyhood and youth accomplished more than could have been expected from the face of it. Hardly a soul is now alive who remembers that we once flew the Blue Eagle in our windows, and fewer still would recall that some earnest people long ago thought the symbol might be the mark of the beast. And only students of twentieth-century European history care that there once was a Benito Mussolini; and they would find it amusing, recalling his humiliating demise, that anyone ever thought he would restore the Roman Empire to its glory, and in the process become the anti-Christ.

But with all of that, and with all the other bizarre and extraordinary sermons that fed my teenage mind, I am grateful for the urgency that this preaching placed in my soul—an urgency that has never really left me. I don't know how real in my teenage years was my expectation that Jesus might return at any moment. But the residual effect is undoubted. Whether I have preached about race relations or conversion, about social justice or sanctification, about personal morality or institutional reform, I have always done so with urgency. I have felt instinctively that the time is short, so I had better be about the Master's business.

Because, you see, it always *is* short. There is never enough time for winning the battle against evil, never enough time for the healing our planet needs, never enough time for working with our Lord to bring his will to pass. That conviction has informed my life. No doubt many factors have made it so; but one of them, without a doubt, is related to those sermons about black shirts, Blue Eagles, Mussolini, and the anti-Christ. Meanwhile, wherever and whatever, I want to be ready when our Lord comes, and I want the same for you. I can't imagine a more urgent matter; and however poorly some evangelists and teachers may have conveyed the idea to me, I'm glad that their point stuck with me. I hope it always will.

5

I'm a Child of the King

WHEN I BECAME THE senior pastor at The Church of the Saviour in Cleveland, Ohio, several of the adult groups asked me to visit their class so they could know me better. One class, made up of persons in my own age group, made the invitation specific. Tell us, they said, those factors that have most influenced your life.

The first two were, as they say, no-brainers: my faith in God and my parents. But the third was almost as easy: the Great Depression. No doubt about it, my experiences beginning in October 1932 are still an everyday influence in my life these seventy-plus years later.

I go back often to that bright fall afternoon when I came home from Hunt School and found my father already home from work. He and my mother and two or three of my older sisters were standing together in the kitchen. It was not a sit-down occasion, and I soon learned why. When I asked my father why he was home early, my mother replied for him. This was not unusual, but this time I suspect that it was merciful. "Daddy's lost his job," she said.

I had no basis for grasping what this meant, but the gravity in the room made everything clear. My father was a laboring man, with no particular skills except integrity and a reasonably strong back. He had driven a delivery truck of one kind or another ever since coming to the city and doing the thing a farmer did best—be a teamster, working with horses. When the horse was replaced by the truck, my father made the move, too. My brothers-in-law sometimes said that he still drove a car or a truck as if it were a wagon. This may well have been true, just as I deal with a computer as if it were still my old Woodstock typewriter.

My father felt no bitterness toward the owner of the laundry. How could he? The times were taking such a bad turn that the owner was now becoming one of the drivers; and since my father's route was the best one, the downtown route, he took it. A good many things aroused my father's disgust—politics, the newspaper, poor preaching—but rarely any bitterness. His example has served me well, even if I haven't reached his level of equanimity.

So what were we to do? My father immediately sought work at the two or three other laundries, but they were no better off than the one he was leaving. He became a freelancer, building his own route from among the most loyal of his customers, using our family car as his delivery truck. The loyal included some personal friends, some houses of ill fame (as we said in those gentler days), and a good number of Negro folks (again, as we said then) in Sioux City's south bottoms. These were the customers who chose the least-expensive method, wet wash or rough dry, and always said cheerfully when Dad picked up the bundle, "Don't bother to bring it, John, until we call you. We'll let you know when we have the money."

Our deeply reduced, very uncertain income meant that we must also find cheaper housing. Like a majority of Americans in that day, we were renters. Some things do change for the better, and here is one of them: An impressive number of people now own their own homes. When I go back to my hometown, Sioux City, Iowa, my pilgrimage takes me to a variety of houses in neighborhoods ranging from marginal to poor, the several houses in which we dwelt in my years of growing up.

We'd been living in a marginal neighborhood, at the edge of a favored school district. Economically, our street didn't rightly belong to Hunt School, and those of us living there knew it. But we also knew that there were great advantages in attending Hunt.

When I went to the principal's office to arrange for my transfer, she looked at what would be our new address. "You're going to be on the line between Irving School and Hobson School," she said thoughtfully. "I'm going to put you in Irving." She made clear that this was much the better choice. Elementary teachers and administrators make so many decisions that are life-shaping. I'm quite sure this was, for me, a crucial one.

Before I leave Hunt School I should tell you that it was there that I last fell in love with a teacher. I don't remember her name, which is surprising; but I can still picture her: a rather tall Jewish woman, strikingly dark; when I think of Queen Esther, I instinctively picture this woman. She never showed any special favors to me (as in fact many teachers did), but I worshiped her from afar. For reasons of full disclosure I should underline that while she was the last schoolteacher I fell in love with, she was not the last unattainable person. I never lost that quality in my dreams, the irrational idea that maybe the person I loved (who of course didn't know I loved her, unless she recognized the bovine eyes that marked me in her presence) would suddenly quit her school, her job, whatever, in order to appear at my door.

I'm not ashamed of this. I think, rather, I would be ashamed if I could not conjure such dreams. Robert Browning said, "Ah, but a man's reach should exceed his grasp, / Or what's a heaven for?" I ponder that most of the lyrics from the great days of Tin Pan Alley, the birthplace of so many songs of fulfilled and unrequited love, were written by men who might not have been seen as typically romantic figures. I think some of them married beautiful women after they became famous, but I suspect they would never have written most of their music if their personal dreams had been fulfilled.

Irving School fit well. At Hunt, I had been, financially, the poorest boy in my class. Now I was in a school where we were all poor (but not as poor, I should add, as were the students in Hobson School). In fact, I had something of an edge in that a substantial number in my class were first-generation Americans, who rarely heard English in their own homes. But like me, they were fervent believers in the American dream. We were passionate achievers.

And Miss Meade called out the best in us. Greek history was a lively subject because so many in the class were of Greek descent. I was not, but my name sounded like it, so I enjoyed fame by association. I remember our running to recess, wondering what would happen the next day between the Greeks and the Trojans. When we studied the Civil War, Miss Meade explained that she was in some way related to General Meade. We were rightly impressed and bragged to our parents about Miss Meade's ties to fame.

We also discussed her wig. It was said that one day, some years past, she had fallen while going from her room to the hall; and her wig had come off, revealing a completely bald head. No one in our class had seen it, but some had heard it on what they insisted was good authority. In our simple day, such stuff made life very exciting. We didn't need television, not when real life had such drama.

I'm often reminded of Miss Meade's wig these days. Sometimes it's via a news story about some political leader or entertainer, or even some literary personality, and sometimes a new book or study about some significant historical figure. It's always a story that shows such a person (as important to the world, or at least to America, as Miss Meade was to us fifth-graders) who has in their past some occasion of appalling fall and baldness. In most instances, because of the preoccupations of our culture, it generally has to do with sex. I trust the data is more substantial than was ours about Miss Meade, though I'm not always sure.

But I ponder. Had we fifth-graders learned from our parents the importance of cutting the admired down to size, to make them manageable? Or is there something in us (original sin, perhaps) that compels us to diminish others—especially larger others? And while one understands fifth-graders snickering over wigs and humiliations, shouldn't humans grow out of this mood when they become adults? And all things considered, are the things that captivate adults any more sophisticated than the fifth-grade fixation on that wig? Mind you, I have nothing but appreciation for the kind of investigative reporting that enforces integrity in our political, religious, and intellectual leaders. And I'd better feel that way, because I've lived all of my life with the Bible, the most honest of all books in its treatment of its heroes. But I suspect we ought to ask ourselves why we are so anxious to find that bigger people have clay feet, and that we ought to decide how much attention such information should receive.

But with all the gains I enjoyed in my new experiences at Irving School, the move was a painful one. Our previous home had been poor, but it was a house in a real neighborhood. Now we moved into the Lee Block, an apartment building of sorts over a series of small businesses. Our apartment was over a bakery, which meant that we shared our lodging with roaches, and of course they outnumbered us exponentially. No running water, we got our water in a pail from a faucet across the hall and drank from a common dipper that was always in the pail. If we were afraid of germs, our fear was soon lost to necessity. There were common bathrooms for men and for women, serving all of the dozen apartments. Whenever I praise the simple life of other days, I omit elements such as these from my consideration.

But the fall from economic grace was nothing like it would be today. The vast mass of Americans lived a simpler life. Here's one obvious example: Those neighborhoods that were built in the 1920s are neighborhoods of one-car garages—or, in such as my family knew, no garage at all, but alleys that led into backyard parking spots. A majority of homes were happy to have one bathroom, not two-and-a-half or three. And the bathroom didn't usually have its own washbasin; one washed and brushed teeth at the kitchen sink, while breakfast was being prepared.

As for brushing teeth, toothpastes were available ("Ipana for the smile of beauty; Sal Hepatica for the smile of health," one favorite radio commercial said cheerfully), but we didn't count on them. Our first-grade teacher told us, during a health class, that if we couldn't afford toothpaste, salt or soda would work just as well. And if homework required glue or paste, we were reminded that we could make our own by mixing a little flour with water. And this was counsel in the pre-Depression years. Economically, life was demonstrably less demanding. Want fun? Get someone's very worn-out automobile tire and roll it down the street. If there was no chalk to make a hopscotch pattern, a piece of soft brick sufficed. And at a certain age, if a boy wanted to have a radio of his own, he bummed a cigar box at the grocery store, spent pennies for some mysterious elements, and made a crystal set—by which, in the quiet of the evening, one could pull a radio program into the bedroom. But it wouldn't be a big-league baseball broadcast because those were all played in the afternoon. And incidentally, there wasn't a big-league team west of St. Louis.

So when the Great Depression came, the fall wasn't as dramatically precipitous as it would be today. Nevertheless, when fully 25 percent of the wage earners were unemployed in an economy where nearly every family had only one employed person, the impact was devastating.

The flip side? It brought out the best in us. I don't think I was a particularly unselfish child, but I remember rising to the occasion on Christmas morning, 1932. We had opened our presents the night before. The best was a jigsaw map of the United States from my sister Phyllis. From my parents, a shirt Mother had made. She was a good seamstress, but a boy doesn't want to wear homemade clothes. But when Mother asked if I liked my presents, I said yes, and said it convincingly, though I was lying. I repeat, I wasn't especially noble; but I was just smart enough to know that my parents were suffering more than I was, and I knew I had to take care of some of that pain.

During the summer that followed, I did still better. I earned occasional pennies selling ice I had picked up each day outside the refrigerator cars on the railroad tracks near our apartment building, and selling popular magazines. *Liberty* magazine cost a nickel, and those of us who sold them got a nickel for each four we sold. Money accumulated slowly, especially for such a poor salesman as I was. But each time I got enough to buy an article of canned goods, I hid it in a box under my bed until the summer day when I presented the bounty to my parents.

This type of experience made me significantly advantaged over any contemporary middle-class child. I was *necessary*. I had demonstrable value. I was more than a consumer, more than a dependent. In truth, of course, what I contributed was so meager as to be ludicrous, but the pride of it was enormous.

I try these days to eat a balanced diet, with an abundance of fruits and vegetables. But I'm a skeptic, even as I do so. My diet in all of my growing-up years was so lacking in balance and nutrients that I should have made my exit long ago. Somehow, though, the food proved adequate and nourishing. The laws of nutrition are all against it, but I and millions of others in my generation are startling evidence of the body's ability to make do with modest supplies.

But the worst pains of poverty are not poor housing or poor food. They're the embarrassment of being different. I didn't feel this pain until I was in junior-high school, because prior to that time, nearly everyone I knew was in the same state. Junior-high schools, taking in larger geographical areas, also encompassed a greater economic variety. My financial limitations became painful when my abilities brought me into the company of students who had so much more. I was the only one of my kind in Latin class, and I soon realized it. I believe many shut themselves out of their own potential because they're afraid to venture among the financially advantaged. I still grow sad at this moment as I recall the loneliness of poverty.

One of my mother's favorite quotations (of which she had an almost endless store) had to do with marriage and poverty. "When poverty comes in the front door, love goes out the side window." Years later, as a pastoral counselor, I learned that while money is not often the major cause of marital discord, it is almost always a contributing factor. For those with enough, money is an issue in its ways of use and distribution; but for the very poor, it is a rancorous, daily issue. There was a day that summer of 1933 when my parents began arguing at the midday meal about family finances. My father seldom raised his voice or said an unkind word, but the pressures had become too great. He threatened to leave. As he got up from the table, I began to cry, and the peas on my fork rolled back on the plate and to the floor. For some people, the picture of poverty is an emaciated baby. For me, it's a boy slobbering into his peas as they roll stupidly underfoot.

I doubt that anyone who didn't experience the poverty of the Great Depression can grasp what it was like. As I have already indicated, in 1932 one of every four workers was unemployed, and in those days this one-in-four figure meant that some 25 percent of American homes were without a breadwinner. There was no unemployment insurance, and relief programs of any kind were almost entirely at the voluntary level.

In my hometown, we didn't have far to fall. It was very much a laboring city with a modest wage base. One evening, one of my brothers-in-law said, "Have you heard what Henry Ford pays his workers there in Detroit? Six dollars a day!" The other men in the room ridiculed the report. No laboring man could possibly make that kind of money. It was easier to believe the other stories, the stories of poverty. Like the evening my father said, "Have you heard what happened at Mook's Café today? A fellow sat down at the counter and asked if he could just have a cup of hot water. The waitress poured it for him, figuring he wanted to warm up. The fellow took a bottle of ketchup, poured some into the cup, stirred it up, and drank it down, thanked the waitress, and went out. Probably his first meal in several days."

The Missouri River separated Sioux City from South Sioux City, Nebraska, and a fair number of people lived in South Sioux and worked in Sioux City. But this meant using the Combination Bridge every day, and walking across it cost five cents each way. In the dead of winter they talked at our house about the people who chose to walk across the river, counting on the ice to hold them, in order to save the nickel. "I wouldn't take that chance," one of the men said. "You would if you needed the nickel bad enough," another one answered.

In desperate times, people prize any kind of work. On evenings several years later as I sat in the far bleachers watching our Sioux City Cowboys play someone in our Class D League, I listened attentively to the men talking around me. I don't know what they paid for their spot on the bench; children under fifteen could join the Knothole Gang and be admitted free. One evening two men sitting nearby were discussing jobs. One man was employed at the site of a building that had recently been torn down.

"What do you do?"

"Scrape bricks. Scrape off the cement so they can be used again."

"Do they pay you by the hour?"

"Nope, it's piece work. I get one cent for each good brick."

"Whadda you make?"

"On a fairly good day, two dollars or a little more."

"Not bad."

It occurs to me that in those days we didn't worry so much about finding places to take our refuse. We reused it. Good stewardship comes easily, without sermons on the environment, when people are so poor that recycling is a way of survival. When I see the current fashion statement of pre-worn jeans, sometimes not only with the color taken from them in the manufacturing process but also with a pre-purchase tear in the knees as well, I ask myself philosophical questions. Why do people want to pay more for clothes that look worn and unkempt? Does such clothing salve the conscience of the middle class, making them feel they are courageous even while they're comfortable? If so, it's a neat trick. Of course most people who dress this way don't know why they do it; they're simply following the path directed by fad and fashion. But I wonder the rationale of the designer who first developed such an unlikely idea. One would have to have exquisite contempt for people's good sense to think they would buy into such a fashion. Probably the designer recognized that you can never underestimate the illogic of people's taste, or the lemming instinct to follow taste once it is stated.

I don't know how some people survived the Depression years. Perhaps it was a variation on the instinct that keeps people going during plagues and famines. But as for the people I knew best, here's what impresses me: They not only survived, they did it with a flourish. The people I knew best went to church. In our church, most of these people were at best marginally employed. Come to think of it, throughout history most of the world's population has lived at such a level. It is only in the past generation or two, in some of the developed world, that a majority or a large minority have lived with enough for tomorrow.

It was humiliating to pull home a coaster wagon of government-surplus food, with its telltale white labels. If I think about it, I can still feel the sting of buying school pants with a county-relief payment slip. My mother was the product of a peasant-woman mother and an upper-middle-class father. ("In the old country, my father's name was not Barth, but *von* Barth," she reminded me at intervals.) So with peasant shrewdness and patrician confidence she would instruct me as we'd go into a store, "Don't tell them we're going to pay for this with a county slip, or they'll try to sell us trash. We'll find what we want, then we'll tell them how we're paying for it."

My parents never protected me from the knowledge of our poverty. I was in on all of the budget discussions. I knew how little we had. Sometimes I was pressed into poverty's service. Our rent at the house where we lived during most of my junior-high and senior-high years was fifteen dollars a month—a challenging sum, when your weekly salary is generally under ten dollars. At especially bad times my parents would hand me seven dollars and fifty cents—half a month's rent, with instruction to take it to the landlord and tell them we'd bring the rest next week. They knew the landlord would accept this from a boy without comment, while if one of them made such a delivery, there would be some sort of showdown.

But I started a few moments ago to say that the people I knew best not only survived, they did so with a flourish. I can see them now, can almost hear them, often closing their eyes as they sang hymns that promised they would "understand it better by and by." They were utterly sure God would see them through.

More than that, they kept their dignity. I find the essence of the matter in one of the hymns most of us knew by heart.

> My Father is rich in houses and land,
> He holdeth the wealth of the world in His hands!
> Of rubies and diamonds, of silver and gold,
> His coffers are full, He has riches untold.

And then, a jubilant refrain:

I'm a child of a King, A child of a King!
With Jesus, my Savior, I'm a child of a King.
(Hattie E. Buell, "The Child of a King," 1877)

At church, we knew this was true. No one could take it from us. Not our landlord, not a storekeeper who preferred better customers, not even the harried welfare workers who sometimes got impatient with the daily helplessness of their charges. I knew I was a child of the King. My clothing didn't show it, our budget denied it, but the facts were there. They were in the Bible, as far as we were concerned, and it was easy to sing them. "With Jesus, my Savior, I'm a child of a King."

I still believe that. And it isn't because I now have money in the bank.

6

From Every Dime, a Penny

IF I STOP AT a drugstore to buy three items—a greeting card, razor blades, and a dark chocolate bar—I may forget all but the dark chocolate bar. But I remember houses and the people who lived in them. So when I make my annual pilgrimage to my hometown, I go not only to the houses in which our family lived, I also find myself identifying some of the houses where childhood playmates lived. I can conjure their pictures and a good share of their names.

I should interrupt myself long enough to say that I don't speak carelessly when I refer to these annual trips as pilgrimages. Some people go to the Lourdes, some to Rome, some to Jerusalem and Bethlehem. I've done some of these too, but my annual pilgrimage is to Sioux City, Iowa. There I thank God for the people who blessed my life in my growing-up years, and there I repent that I haven't done better with what those good, kind, probably very ordinary people invested in me.

But back to those houses. On my last pilgrimage I sought out not only the homes in which our family lived; I also located the home of Hulda and Caroline Weintz. They were sisters who never married. I realized on this visit that their home was quite small, but of course all of us lived in smaller homes in the 1930s; students of architecture or of real estate can give you the square-foot statistics. Some of my friends have walk-in closets bigger than any bedroom I knew in my boyhood.

From the outside, Hulda's and Caroline's house isn't as neatly kept as I remember it, but of course it's two generations older now. I remember it from my several ventures as an entrepreneur, specifically from those times when I tried selling magazines from door to door. I have no idea why I kept thinking I could sell anything. I went to each door praying no one would be there, which is a very bad attitude when you're on commission sales. When I would return home quite defeated with my full inventory of magazines, Mother would say, "Go to the Weintz sisters. They'll buy one from you."

And they always did. It was part of their kindly nature. They would look over my two or three possibilities—*Liberty, Delineator, Pictorial Review*—and would find something in one of them that justified a purchase. I know now that though they were no doubt enthusiastic readers, they were more particularly generous human beings. The Kalas boy needed a sale, so they would buy.

This generosity was the essence of who those women were. And it is to that quality that I am eternally (I'm using the word quite intentionally) indebted. Hulda Weintz was my Sunday school teacher in that autumn of 1933 when I became a Christian, and she taught me to tithe. I don't remember the case she made. No doubt it was quite simple; as simple, in fact, as this, that this is what the Bible teaches. In that day, ten-year-olds were impressed by authority, and we knew the Bible was the ultimate authority, with our Sunday school teacher running a respectable second. Miss Weintz also broke down the economics, making the whole idea manageable: For every dime we earned or were given, we should give a penny to God.

I have said earlier that it is quite difficult to translate the economy of that place and period to our time, but here's what Hulda Weintz's message meant to me. In those days *Liberty* magazine— one of the popular Big Three, along with *Collier's* and *The Saturday Evening Post*—sold for five cents a copy. Those of us who sold them from door to door were paid a nickel for every four copies we sold; thus, to earn a dime, one sold eight copies of *Liberty* magazine. Those (like my friend Hookey Shapiro) who hawked newspapers on downtown streets, did better. The papers sold for three cents, and they made a penny on each sale.

So Hulda Weintz taught me to tithe. I'm sure she told our class something about how much good the money would do, and how even our small gifts would be far-reaching, and how the money and our very lives belonged to God anyway, so we'd better be giving our tithe, but I don't really remember any of that. And although I recall her teaching a tithing lesson only once, I have no doubt she reinforced the matter on other occasions, with the kind of supporting word here and there that preachers and teachers so often employ. And I was convinced.

Of course I was ready to be convinced. I was a new convert, and I wanted nothing so much as to do what my Lord wanted of me. I suspect this is also why in that same period I so readily accepted a call to Christian service. I wish that I might always have a heart as tender to God's purposes as was the case in those simple days, the heart of someone newly in love with God. It was really quite easy to begin tithing at that early point in my Christian walk. I was young enough in my faith to know that eternity matters, *really* matters, and that people matter—and that money, which on the whole is so transient, can play a part in eternal affairs.

Many years later, as a pastor in Cleveland, Ohio, I had reason to contemplate the values of an early conversion to tithing. After I had preached on tithing one Sunday morning, one of my most loyal families paused an extra moment to thank me for the sermon. The man was the chief executive officer of a major corporation, with the kind of salary that meant his name and salary and stock benefits were sometimes listed in business and management publications. They said that they wished their son, who was then a university student, had been there to hear the sermon. They wanted him to tithe, as they did, and they felt the importance of starting early. The executive made the point quite simply. "If we hadn't started tithing when I was a clerk making twenty dollars a week, I doubt that we could do so now. The figures now would seem so big!"

I found that interesting and in a way amusing, because I thought of the scores (perhaps hundreds) of times I had heard people say, "If only I had so-and-so's money," or "if only we had a bigger income," they would begin tithing. It doesn't work that way. We enlarge the boundaries of our sense of limitation to accommodate our lifestyle. Remember the old fable about the man who said he could lift an ox, and who did so by beginning with a newborn calf, lifting it every day so that his strength grew with the weight of the animal? The principle applies to tithing. It's good to start young.

Not long ago one of my former students told me the wonderful story of his parents, who in comfortable executive retirement began doing short-term mission projects in Central or South America. When they saw the poverty in which so many were living, they moved from their substantial home to a more modest one, so they could give more—and because they felt the incongruity of living so impossibly above the people to whom they now minister several months of the year. I was moved to incoherence by the story, but I mumbled something to the effect, "You know, that's a conversion too. When you're fifty, sixty, seventy years old, you have to be born again—again—to make such a change in your finances."

So I'm grateful that with Hulda Weintz's help I began to tithe as a ten-year-old. I saved up that first tithe for many weeks until I had seventeen cents. (As you can see, I remember the figure precisely.) I had always contributed to the Sunday school offering—a penny or sometimes two, and rarely a nickel. But this had been money my parents had given me for the purpose. Now that I had begun tithing, I realized that those earlier contributions had been my parents' gifts, not mine. The seventeen cents, however, was an entirely other matter. I suspect I have never since had such a feeling of grandeur in giving. Students of New Testament Greek sometimes remind us that 2 Corinthians 9:7 ("for God loves a cheerful giver") could rightly be translated, "for God loves a *hilarious* giver." I came pretty close to the "hilarious" category that Sunday morning in the basement of the Helping Hand Mission when I deposited my seventeen cents.

I'm not sure what my parents thought of my commitment to tithing. At the time, they gave in rather nominal fashion, probably like a majority of church members, including some of the most faithful and most involved. No doubt much of what was going on in my life those days must have made them ponder. Mind you, I was a normal ten-year-old, going to school, playing pick-up football games after school, listening to the radio with my parents in the evenings. But my life had found a new center in Christ, and that center now included the way I looked at money.

It was four or five years later that my parents began to tithe. At our house, as in the homes of most of the people we knew, the Great Depression was still in control. I don't know what caused my parents at that time, when their own finances were so continually precarious, to commit themselves to tithing. Clearly, it was a bigger step for them in their circumstances than for a boy whose income was without demands. Their decision was a result of their unfolding walk with Christ, and it called for great faith. At that particular time, my father was on salary at a laundry, making nine dollars a week, and occasionally a little more by way of commissions. The three of us sat around the table on Tuesday evenings while mother distributed the money: thirty cents for life insurance, three dollars and fifty cents toward the rent, ninety cents for the tithe. Yes, my parents must have had deep conviction and commitment to take on tithing under such circumstances.

Hulda Weintz, who was my teacher for probably only six months, left me with other benefits too. It was she who explained that the Book of Psalms was a book of poetry. I remember feeling rather sorry for her when she gave us this word, because I knew what poetry was—lines that rollicked along with a certain rhythm and that employed closing rhymes. There was nothing of that in the psalms of our King James Bible. Only many years later did I learn that Miss Weintz was right, and that the psalms were indeed poetry, as are also Job, Proverbs, Ecclesiastes, and many of the books of the prophets.

She had us memorize many Bible verses, of course; that was standard operating procedure in those days, and I confess without apology that I'm grateful for it. One verse stands out, because I can still picture this doughty little woman reciting the verse as if she were standing with Martin Luther at the Diet of Worms.

"Then Peter and the other apostles answered and said, We ought to obey God rather than men" (Acts 5:29, KJV). She intended for us to display our courage on the playground, on the way home from school, and wherever else someone might challenge our faith or our conduct. In my adult life I have had opportunity to speak under the aegis of that verse in a variety of other occasions that would not have occurred to Miss Weintz when she taught us, including a variety of city council meetings and state legislative committees and newspaper columns that brought me anonymous hate mail. She believed we should be ready to stand up and be counted, and she was right. By our very calling, we Christians are a check and balance to the culture around us. God have mercy on us if we sometimes forget that "we ought to obey God rather than men."

But from a purely pragmatic point of view, the biggest thing that sixth-grade Sunday school teacher did for me was to establish me in a lifetime investment program. As a result, I now have investments in elementary schools in Africa and the islands of the sea, colleges and theological seminaries in America and abroad, homes for the aging and hospitals in several parts of the world. And, yes, rescue missions in several large cities, food distribution centers for the poor, and summer camps for children.

And people! Above all, I have investments in people, both living and dead! I can't tell you how exciting that is. Some of those people I know or have known because I was giving directly to the person or to the enterprise that employed the person. But the vast number of them I have never seen and cannot begin to imagine, ranging from a blur of faces in Africa to unknown college and seminary students whose scholarships I've been part of. I couldn't feel this rich if I had major holdings in the world's top fifty corporations.

Don't think, however, that I am so starry-eyed about this matter that I think I've won on every investment. I know better than that. Some of the churches to which I gave money are long since closed, and some of the people I've invested in seem to have forsaken the faith they once espoused. I know of scores of colleges and theological seminaries that live on endowments that earnest persons gave out of convictions that those institutions now deny, sometimes by neglect and other times by candid statement. In the world of business, people sometimes speak of stock certificates that aren't even worth using as wallpaper. I suspect there's some equivalent statement that could be made for some of the money— and time and prayers too—that I've given to institutions and individuals. I feel bad about this, but undefeated. I believe simply and wholeheartedly in the purposes of God, so much so that I'm confident God will bring some eternal good out of even the worst of my holy investments.

Please understand me. There's nothing remotely heroic about what I've done with my giving through this more than half a century. It's as simple as Hulda Weintz taught us: For every dime you get, take out a penny for God and others. What could be easier? And what could be more far-reaching? That's why I said earlier that I'm *eternally* (remember the word?) grateful for what Miss Weintz taught our class of boys at the Helping Hand Mission.

7

How Can You Be a
Preacher If You Haven't
Read the Bible Through?

O
UR HEROIC FIGURES come in a variety of styles and
sizes. As a typical boy of my era—and probably of any
era—I had sports heroes. I made Rogers Hornsby my
object of baseball adulation, which then required me to cheer for
the team he managed, the long-since-forgotten St. Louis
Browns—an experience that got me started in a lifelong pattern of
endorsing underdogs. And there was the legendary heavyweight
champion Jack Dempsey, such an icon that during the time I lived
in New York City years later I delighted in having lunch at the
Great Northern Hotel, so I could pass by his desk in the lobby and
have him smile and say hello as if he actually knew me. But as
I've already told you, the continuing heroes of my boyhood were
preachers, small and large, famous and unknown. In my eyes,
they were all great.

Especially Gene Palmer. Thank God for Gene Palmer! I can
picture his face even as I write, but if I should doubt my memory,
I still have a newspaper clipping in a scrapbook that contains pictures of a variety of other preacher-heroes—both men and

women, because a fair number of evangelists in my youth were women. There was a bit of rotundity in Gene Palmer, from his smile to his waistline. He smiled easily and warmly, in a way that made one feel he would be in danger if he had to restrain that smile for too long. In basic contours, I see Gene Palmer each Christmas season in Clarence the angel, from the seasonal classic *It's a Wonderful Life*—except that Clarence wears a continually apprehensive look while Gene Palmer's expression was just as continually at peace—with God, with life, and with his fellow human beings. Oh, yes, and he wore bow ties that matched his smile.

He was a Presbyterian evangelist, and our little Methodist church had engaged him to preach a series of revival services— two weeks, if my memory is right. His claim to a hearing was two-fold: He was a gambler before his conversion, and he was converted in a Billy Sunday revival. And another thing: Each evening just before his sermon he did a magic trick, to make some moral point. I still remember the night he held in his hand a large, empty fruit can into which he dropped a series of separate chain links, while the audience called out at his request the names of some bad habits. Just a *little* bad, he emphasized, not seriously bad—not enough, that is, really to hurt someone. But then (talking steadily even as we watched), he pulled out of the can a chain, a full-grown chain. Those little things, he said, don't amount to anything by themselves, but they'll tie you up someday.

We boys adored him. I remember that Jackie Caylor and I went to him after a church service so I could seek his help on a major moral issue: Was it gambling to play marbles for keeps? He explained gently that it probably wasn't a sin, but that when he was a boy he got into gambling early because he and his buddies added to the excitement by putting coins under the marbles. If you and I were talking rather than my putting all this into writing, I'd ask you if you'd like to hear some of the stories he told, but I have to confess that their appeal is more to the antiquarian than to the student of religion or literature. In truth, where some people collect physical antiques, others of us enjoy the intellectual or sociological equivalent. Unfortunately, there's no market for these anecdotal antiques, though they're no more lacking in beauty or substance than some of the things I see in most antique shops.

On the last Sunday of Gene Palmer's revival services, he came to our home for Sunday dinner. In the course of the meal my mother announced proudly that I had a call to the ministry. Although this was a very settled matter in my soul, I hadn't intended to go public so early. Now here is the first eternally great thing about Gene Palmer: He took that news seriously. When we had finished eating, he excused himself from the adults because, he said, he wanted to talk with this boy about his call. There in a corner of a not-very-large living room, he said a number of serious things to me, of which I remember just one. I count it one of the two or three most life-shaping experiences of all my years.

I've told the story so many times that I hesitate to do so now, lest you've heard me somewhere. Nevertheless, here goes— because this conversation is what this chapter is all about.

"Have you read the Bible through yet?"

"Uh-huh, I read the Bible."

"No, I asked if you've read it *through.*"

"*All the way?*"

"All the way! How can you hope to be a preacher if you haven't read the Bible through?"

Gene Palmer then gave me a method, one that appealed to a boy just turning eleven, because it was manageable. You eat an elephant one bite at a time, and the Bible I owned certainly seemed to be of elephant-proportions. Read three chapters every weekday, Mr. Palmer told me, and five chapters every Sunday, and you'll finish the entire Bible in a year.

I resolved to start immediately. But we were already several weeks into 1934, and something structured and disciplined in my personality made me want to finish the Bible not simply in a year's time, but in that particular calendar year. So that night I re-calculated the formula for my immediate purposes. How could I finish the 1,189 chapters of the Bible within 1934? I could still work with three chapters on weekdays if I did nine chapters every Sunday.

And I did. I finished my journey through the Bible that year. And the next year, and the next, and the next. I have no idea how many times I've read the Bible through in my lifetime. At the moment of this writing, I am in an "off year"—that is, a year in which I am reading more intensively in selected portions of the Bible. But next year, the Lord willing, I intend to start on the annual journey once again.

Some years ago I told this story at a Bible training conference where I was speaking. A co-leader in the conference responded in his session by commenting that he didn't know why someone would want to read the Bible through a number of times; he felt there were portions that weren't worth reading even once. I knew he was having fun at my expense, but I also knew that he was serious in his feeling that some parts of the Bible are a waste of time. I think by contrast of William Tyndale, whose translation of a portion of the Old Testament is part of my reading this year. Tyndale was not only one of the most learned men of his century, he was a scholar who could hold his own in any generation. When a fellow scholar mocked Tyndale's plan to translate the Bible into the English vernacular, Tyndale replied, "If God spare my life, ere many years I will cause a boy that driveth a plow shall know more of the Scripture than thou dost." Eventually Tyndale was strangled to death for his efforts at translating the Bible, and his body burned. He didn't pick and choose as to which parts were worth translating and which not; if he had, I suspect he would have completed the psalms before his martyrdom, rather than the chapters in First Chronicles that seem pretty tedious to the average reader.

I admit readily that I enjoy some parts of the Bible more than others. I prefer the Gospel of Luke to the Book of Numbers, and First Corinthians captures more of me than Second Kings. But I'm grateful that Gene Palmer told me a preacher must read all of the Bible. There is a sense in which one can't really appreciate the total plot unless one reads the whole book; and indeed, unless one reads it from beginning to end. In saying this I identify myself as having limited sympathy with those Bible-reading plans that include in each day's reading a potpourri of Pentateuch, psalms, Gospels, and epistles. One can say at the end of such a year's reading that he has read the whole Bible, but one can't hope to have grasped the grand themes that weave through the Book in such a fascinating and sometimes intricate way.

The Bible is like any other truly great friendship; one needs to know it warts and all. Some (including some who have never read the whole Bible) will think I'm irreverent in what I've just said. If so, it is the irreverence of honesty. The Bible is a very uneven book. There is nothing in all of literature grander than "In the beginning was the Word, and the Word was with God, and the Word was God" (John 1:1). On the other hand, it's hard to feel the same excitement for "The descendants of Japheth: Gomer, Magog, Madai, Javan, Tubal, Meshech, and Tiras" (1 Chronicles 1:5). But both verses have their place in the plotline, so I still subscribe to the question/conviction with which Gene Palmer pinned me to the wall: "How can you be a preacher if you haven't read the Bible through?"

Now and then as I lecture and preach around the country someone will introduce me as "a great biblical scholar." This embarrasses me to no end, not only because I'm unhappy with the quality of hype and promotion that has taken over the church in the past two decades but also because I know how far I am from being a biblical scholar. I confess to my embarrassment that I know nothing of Hebrew, which one ought to know if one is to be an Old Testament scholar. And to my shame I confess that though I've taken a good deal of New Testament Greek, I've allowed my knowledge of the language to slip entirely from me.

What I am is a person who loves the Bible. I began to fall in love with it the day I embarked on Gene Palmer's regimen for the first time, although Sunday school teachers like Laura Olson and Hulda Weintz had already given me a good start. Seven decades later, the love affair is stronger than ever. Every day, right after my morning ablutions, I read the Bible; and every day I find something new. And before some wiseacre tells me that he's known someone who was equally slow in math or geography, I rise to say that the newness is a result of the depth of the material and the quite wonderful way the Holy Spirit adapts it to the changing patterns of my life.

I served four churches during the thirty-eight years that I was a pastor, and in each place I preached a sermon early in my pastorate—usually in late December, for obvious reasons—challenging my people to read the Bible through on the three-by-five method. A great many people of all ages have responded to my urging. I think especially of a wonderful woman in her eighties who told me apologetically that she had been a Christian since she was a little girl and had never made this grand trip, but that she was going to do so now. She was fearful she wouldn't live out the year. Nearly every Sunday while leaving worship, she reported where she now stood in her reading—and always with the fervent word, "I just hope I live out this year, so I can finish." She did.

Some twenty-five years after that February Sunday when Gene Palmer got me started on my lifelong Bible journey, I learned that he was still alive and that he was employed by—most appropriately!—one of the great Bible societies. Life offers few greater joys than the chance to pay a long-overdue debt of thanks, so I wrote him to tell him that I was now a pastor and that I was carrying on his three-by-five Bible regimen in the churches I served. He replied immediately. I doubt that he remembered me; a traveling evangelist met many ten- and eleven-year-old boys in the course of his work. But he was pleased to hear, no doubt about it. And he told me that he had upped the standard for himself, so that now he was reading the Bible at a more rapid pace, several times a year.

I wish he were alive still, so I might tell him what has happened in more recent years. After my book *Parables from the Back Side* had been in publication long enough that it appeared I might be worth a second chance, my editor at the time asked me if I had an idea for a second book. I told her about my pattern of Bible reading, and my idea for building a devotional book around the daily readings. Abingdon Press agreed that it was worth trying. After several years, another Abingdon editor told me that the book needed to be part of a larger project, which she named *The Grand Sweep*. So I wrote two companion volumes—one a study guide and the other a book of sermon ideas for pastors who wanted to preach through the Bible in a year while the people in their congregations were in the reading project. I also recorded an audio version of the entire Bible with the devotional for each day, for the benefit of those who have vision problems or who want to have devotional time while walking, jogging, or commuting to work. Many thousands of persons have now gone through the Bible as a result of this additional project. Thank you, Gene Palmer! I am grateful no end for the chance to carry on the afternoon conversation you invested in me.

But it's more than *The Grand Sweep.* All of the more than thirty books I've written—and the other books, please God, that I may still write—are a product of my lifetime of Bible reading. I've read the Bible enough to know when I should smile, because the Bible has many funny stories and most religious people miss them because—not knowing the Bible well—they think they should approach it with a proper sense of the somber. They don't realize that some of the most serious matters can be understood only if they're told with a grin.

I've also read the Bible enough to have joined the neighborhood and sometimes the families of its characters. I hurt for that scoundrel Cain when he wants to build a city named for his son (Genesis 4:17). I smile when Balaam makes a fool of himself over his suddenly intelligent donkey. When the psalmist prays in his confession of sin, "Do not cast me away from your presence, / and do not take your holy spirit from me" (Psalm 51:11), I feel that he wrote the words for me; I am his nearest kin in that prayer. And when John envisions a day when a trumpet will sound and loud voices in heaven will say, "The kingdom of the world has become the kingdom of our Lord / and of his Messiah, / and he will reign forever and ever" (Revelation 11:15), my soul answers, "Yes! Amen! You have my vote!"

Thank you, Gene Palmer, for slipping away from the adult conversation that winter Sunday afternoon to ask a boy, "How can you be a preacher if you haven't read the Bible through?" You challenged me right into a lifetime of beauty and wonder.

8

Promises Are for Believers

WHEN I MAKE MY annual pilgrimage to Sioux City and its environs, I include a wide variety of stops. Each has its unique claim on my soul, allowing me to trace the unfolding of my Christian journey by street and by neighborhood. But no stop is as significant as West Palmer Street. As I walk through the area now, I realize that it was really quite pleasant. Our house was clearly the poorest in the several blocks, a duplex with no redeeming qualities, heated on the main floor by a coal stove and for the bedrooms on the second floor by a square-foot floor register that was intended to coax heat from the first floor. On Iowa winter mornings, I learned early to put on my socks before stepping out of bed onto the linoleum. We talked in those days about Jack Frost painting the windows. He had a full, two-story art gallery many winter days at that West Palmer address.

It was while we were living in this home that I became a Christian, recognized my call to the ministry, began tithing, and began reading the Bible through for the first time. It was also in this house that I learned something fundamental about the promises of the Holy Scriptures.

I suppose there was hardly a devout home in those days that didn't have a "precious promise box." In most instances this was a little cardboard container holding some sixty or eighty cards, each measuring perhaps one inch by four inches. On each card was printed a Bible verse that was intended to convey comfort, strength, or hope—"precious promises," indeed. My mother kept our box on a kitchen shelf where she could take one each morning. Sometimes she found something mystical in the card she drew, because it seemed to her to have particular significance for that day or for some circumstance in her life—a coincidence that a cynic would have found amusing but that was deeply satisfying to my mother. But whether or not the drawn-by-chance Scripture verse had apparent connection for the day, it was always a source of strength for my mother, preparing her for the fortunes of the day.

I'm thinking just now of a cold morning in late November or early December of 1933. A few weeks earlier, my sister Phyllis had borne her first child, a beautiful little girl. In the pattern of those days, she stayed in the hospital the usual five days, then was brought home in an ambulance. A few days later she was discovered to be with scarlet fever.

The city health officer immediately quarantined our home. This meant that a sign was nailed to our front door, warning that a contagious disease had afflicted someone in the house and that no one outside the family should enter. I learned many years later that such a quarantine was first imposed in 1348, in Italy. With the people of Venice dying from a plague at a rate of six hundred a day, the city government imposed a quarantine on travelers from the Orient. For how long? They chose forty days, symbolizing the period Jesus spent in the wilderness after his baptism, and for the forty named the period *quaranta giorni*, from which we get our English word *quarantine*.

At the same time the health officer moved Phyllis to an isolation hospital on the edge of the city where they kept persons with infectious diseases. In the crude language of those days we called it "the pest house," because people with a pestilence were kept there. On this particular morning, the hospital telephoned our next-door neighbors—like most of the poor in those days, we had no telephone—to tell us that Phyllis was dying. Now the three of us—Mother, Phyllis's husband, Marlowe, and I—

shivered on the sidewalk, so that as soon as my father drove up with the laundry truck, we could climb in and be on our way without delay, hoping we would get to the hospital before our loved one died.

But my mother had told me something earlier that morning. "It says in the Ninety-first Psalm," she said, " 'There shall no evil befall thee, neither shall any plague come nigh thy dwelling' " (Psalm 91:10, KJV). There was another verse in the same chapter that had also enheartened her: "A thousand shall fall at thy side, and ten thousand at thy right hand; but it shall not come nigh thee" (91:7, KJV). This was my mother's confidence. It accompanied us to the pest house, and for the perilous days that followed, and then through recovery. Yes, my sister lived; lived, in fact, into her eighties.

But suppose Phyllis had died? Suppose the promise of Psalm 91 had failed? Many of us have known someone who prayed in a time of crisis; and when the prayer was not answered, they concluded that prayer doesn't work and that the Bible isn't true, and therefore they want nothing more to do with religion. Some students of biography and literature say that Ralph Waldo Emerson's attitude toward religion took a decided turn after the death of his young wife. This has been the case with great numbers of people, who felt as a result of the Holocaust that there could be no God, or that if there were, such a God didn't really matter.

Nor does it have to be such a crucial, life-and-death matter. Think of all those people who have prayed for a certain job and didn't get it, or who believed that a particular house was just right for them but their prayer didn't bring it to pass, or—especially— those persons who have fallen in love and have been sure that this is the person whose place in their lives would make them happy and who told God so, but it didn't help. Most of them can quote a Bible verse to buttress their issue, or at least something that sounds like a Bible verse. "Ask, and it will be given you" (Matthew 7:7); they asked, and it wasn't given. "If in my name you ask me for anything," Jesus said, "I will do it" (John 14:14); they were careful to make their request in Jesus' name, but they didn't get the answer they wanted. "If two of you shall agree on earth as touching any thing that they shall ask, it shall be done for them of my Father which is in heaven" (Matthew 18:19, KJV). We agreed, someone says, and we prayed for months, but it was not done.

So what about these promises? Are they true?

Yes, they're true. The Bible's promises are true. But the promises are for believers.

I know that at this moment some reader is getting angry with me. You're saying (and wishing you could say it to me in person), "I'm a believer, and just as good a believer as you or your mother, but it hasn't worked for me." Believe me, I don't mean to challenge you at that point. I will concede readily that your quality of believing is probably just as good as mine. Someone else feels I'm being very elitist, suggesting that God listens only to the super pious. I surely don't want to leave you with that opinion, because there's nothing intentionally of the super pious in me, and I hate elitism in religion as much as you do.

But let me remind you of a story from the life of Jesus. Just after Jesus was baptized by John, he went out into the wilderness, where he fasted for forty days. Twice Satan tempted Jesus in special ways, and twice Jesus answered with Scripture. Then Satan used a different tack: He quoted scripture to Jesus. He challenged Jesus to cast himself down from a pinnacle of the Temple, and he made his point by quoting from the very psalm that meant so much to my mother on that bitter winter morning. "For it is written," Satan said, "[God] shall give his angels charge over thee, to keep thee: And in their hands they shall bear thee up, lest at any time thou dash thy foot against a stone" (Luke 4:10-11, KJV). That is, Satan was saying to Jesus, "Test God's promise. Let's see if it works for you."

The Gospel writer tells us that Jesus refused to throw himself from the pinnacle of the Temple. Specifically, Jesus said that to do what Satan suggested would be to "tempt the Lord." In a broad yet definitive sense, Jesus was saying that God's promises are not to be used promiscuously or carelessly, but very thoughtfully. In truth, Satan seemed to be working on the logical argument that this was a good time for Jesus to prove the scriptures.

To do so at that moment would be to credential Jesus' ministry in a powerful, almost irrefutable way. A miracle coming at this time following Jesus' baptism would give Jesus a platform of faith on which to embark upon his ministry. But Jesus didn't reason that way. His answer to the Tempter was forthright and without equivocation: The promises of God are sacred and shouldn't be used casually.

Now, here's what I'm trying to say: Only believers take such an attitude toward the promises of God. Our natural attitude is to treat God like an errand boy—particularly, an errand boy that we think about primarily when we need a favor. And if at such a time God doesn't provide the service we request (indeed, insist upon), we look for some other errand and delivery service. When Jesus said, "Don't tempt the Lord your God," it was like saying, "You shall not treat the Lord God casually and capriciously."

So I'm putting special content into the word *believer* when I say that promises are for believers. I am speaking of the kind of believing that realizes that the ultimate issue and the ultimate promise is *God*, which means that we are ready to let God be God. When we look at God and the promises of God in this fashion, we are trusting that whatever happens, matters will eventually turn out right because God is God, and therefore God will—in one way or another—bring about the ultimate, eternal right.

That is, such a believer doesn't believe in God because certain promises have come true; he or she believes in the character and wisdom of God. The promises—and the way they turn out in our lives—are not the issue; God is the issue. If the promises seem to fail, no matter, there is still *God*.

This is the kind of belief demonstrated for us in a wonderful little story in the Old Testament Book of Daniel. Shadrach, Meshach, and Abednego, three young Hebrew boys, probably only teenagers or a little more, were ordered to bow down to an image set up by the king. Of course if they did so, they would by that act deny the Lord God. They refused to bow down, so an order was given for their execution via a fiery furnace. The king challenged the young men: Who, then, "is the god that will deliver you out of my hands?"

The young men answered the king respectfully but emphatically. "[W]e have no need to present a defense to you in this matter. If our God whom we serve is able to deliver us from the furnace of blazing fire and out of your hand, O king, let him deliver us. But if not, be it known to you, O king, that we will not serve your gods and we will not worship the golden statue that you have set up" (Daniel 3:16-18).

"But if not"! The three young men were confident of God's ability to deliver them, and ready to trust that confidence, but they didn't see this as the end of the matter. If God didn't deliver them, their belief was unchanged. This was because their belief was in God, and in the righteousness that God represented; their belief was not in God's promises, but in God.

Another wonderful Old Testament personality, Job, gives us the same kind of answer, marked by the same kind of believing. Perhaps you remember his story. He was a person who had everything: family, money, position, community respect. Still more, he was a thoroughly good human being, blessed by God. But then, in a series of irrational disasters, he lost everything, or almost everything. His wealth, his children, then his health, and with all of that, his standing in the community—because his was a world where people assumed that if you suffered ill fortune, it was a sign you were morally flawed. His wife felt that his best out was to curse God and die—a kind of holy mercy killing. Job still had a few friends, but with friends like his, enemies were superfluous. They comforted him, essentially, by telling him he was getting what he deserved. Then, worst of all, it seemed to Job that even God had turned against him. The promises of God? There was no such thing.

Job struggled with the bitter anomaly. He railed against God and pleaded for a chance to state his case with the Eternal, in hopes of getting a fair trial. Yet from the pit of his hopelessness, Job dared to cry, "Though he slay me, yet will I trust in him" (Job 13:15, KJV).

During those dark winter days, when it seemed certain a very young mother would die, I began to deal with ambiguity, though I surely didn't know that word at the time. I was being privileged to get beyond bumper-sticker religion and praise-chorus happiness. Life is not simple, and our relationship with God is not simple. Nor are the promises of God. At first reading, they seem so all-encompassing: "Only believe." "All things are possible to those who believe." "Agree, two of you, and it shall be done."

These are magnificent promises. As pastor and friend, I have quoted them to a great many people, and I have fiercely clasped them to my own soul in dark days. But I am grateful that I learned early that a fact is brooding behind the promises and that this brooding fact is God. I learned to say, "You are God, and I am not. If the promises do not work, nothing ultimate has changed. Absolutely nothing. You, O God, remain." If I do not understand why my very reasonable prayers seem ignored or why an unworthy person prospers while a good one suffers, still there is God. I began even then to realize that the greatest biblical promise is not "All things are possible to those who believe," or even "And we know that in everything God works for our good." No; the greatest promise is *God.* And if God be God, and if I am at peace with that fact, in time the promises will take care of themselves.

So my sister Phyllis lived. But what if she hadn't? What if, that day, we had gotten to the pest house just in time to watch her die? What would have happened then to my mother's faith?

Not a thing, I'm quite sure of it. You see, even that morning, as a ten-year-old, I saw the incongruity of what my mother was telling me. She was quoting a scripture that said no plague would come nigh our dwelling. But the plague had already come to our duplex on West Palmer Street. Phyllis was in detention, and there was a quarantine sign on our house, as Mother very well knew. The plague was in our dwelling, and a quarantine sign announced it to all who walked by.

But somehow my mother knew that none of this mattered. If the plague was there, this scarlet fever of death, she was moving to the next line in the promise, that death would not come. And if that had not worked and death had come, she would have gone to the next line. She would have gone to God.

I learned that winter that God must be our bottom line. To be specific, our confidence in the character of God. I love the promises of Scripture, as I've already said, and I would encourage anyone to memorize them and to quote them in the face of hell. But remember that the ultimate promise is God. And if all the promises sometimes seem to fail, *still* there is God. Always, there is God.

A Summing Up

A TUNE AND A fragment of a lyric keep playing in my mind just now. It was a popular ballad some years ago, but all I can remember just now is the signature phrase: "It was a very good year . . ." It's appropriate that this phrase should play so insistently in my mind as I complete this story.

Because of course that's what this little book is all about. And as you no doubt sense at this point, it isn't just a very good year that I've been recalling, but the year that launched my life: Everything I know about myself—as a person, a Christian, a preacher, a writer, a handler of money, and a quite-imperfect human being—dates back to that year that began in the fall of 1932 and continued into February of 1934. I have learned hundreds of lessons since then, many of them from the sins I've committed and from the arrogance that has sometimes led me astray; but all of those lessons are sub-studies of that tenth year. I have preached thousands of sermons and have now written more than thirty books, but the genetic code for it all is in that little collection of months. I'd like to hope that through the years of my life I've been able to help some people; if so, it is the product of the decisions made during that year and the goodness that numbers of people invested in me.

I've said a good deal in this book about the Great Depression and about being poor. I hope you sense that there is no anger or complaint in these references. Now and then when I'm talking with someone else from my generation, they will say to me, "We were poor, but we didn't know it, because everyone was poor in those days." I sometimes agree with them, cheerfully, but I'm lying. I knew we were poor. To be honest, I don't think those people who say "we didn't know it" were really poor. Because, you see, you know you're poor if you get some of your clothing from a relief center, and if you pull home a coaster wagon of the white-labeled surplus foods, and if you can't go to the dime assembly in the junior-high auditorium because you can't afford a dime for admission.

I won't tell you that it didn't hurt when I was going through it. But somehow the pain never got too deep, largely because my parents took me so fully into their confidences about our family finances. I knew how bad off we were. I was a full partner in the perilous enterprise.

I don't want to be piously philosophical about all of this, but I've benefited all of my life from the limitations of my growing-up years. I think one can learn—at least in the United States of America—how to be at home in a more sophisticated intellectual, financial, or cultural milieu; but one can understand being poor only by growing up in it. I know enough about poverty that I don't romanticize it, but I also know that it isn't as easy to pull oneself up by the bootstraps as some of the middle-class-comfortable love to say.

I know too that I had some advantages that others in my economic class didn't have. I was bright enough that adults—especially my teachers and Christian friends—encouraged me. I was hopelessly awkward on the playground (to my huge disappointment at the time), but I was graceful in classroom discussions. I didn't survive even the first cut when I went out for the football and basketball teams at Central High School, but this meant that I gave my full energy to the debate team and to the *a cappella* choir—matters far, far more valuable to me in the years since then.

And how I thank God for people! I've mentioned only a few by name; but if I didn't restrain myself, this postscript would read like the opening chapters of First Chronicles. When I make my annual pilgrimages to Northwest Iowa, I speak scores of these names to God. Every year I recall some names I haven't mentioned before. My debt to people is eternal—including some people who meant me ill, but whose words or conduct proved ultimately to my good.

In the midst of writing this book I accompanied a group of my students on a five-day retreat to a famous abbey. I was blessed by the prayers seven times a day and by the silence; in truth, I would have been glad for still more silence. The grounds were beautiful, and I was lifted by the knowledge that ten thousands of hours of prayer have arisen from that setting.

But as I left the abbey, I realized I'd rather go to Sioux City. The town of my birth (both physical and spiritual) reminds me, for better and for worse, of who I am. I remember people, my body of saints. And sinners too, including myself. And I remember God, my Faithful Lord, who has pursued me untiringly over the years.

This is not because I am out of the ordinary. Anyone who reads this book could construct his or her own house of gratitude, with lines just as fine as mine. It is the wonder, the miracle of life—*any* Life—that it has the potential of going from biography to pilgrimage. The secret is in God and in knowing our destination.

Amen. Thanks be to God.

Discussion Guide for

What I Learned When I Was Ten,

by J. Ellsworth Kalas

John D. Schroeder

In this book popular author J. Ellsworth Kalas reflects on the tenth year of his life, and how that particular year shaped him and his Christian faith in a number of important ways. He shares stories about what it was like growing up in Sioux City, Iowa, during the days of the Great Depression; and he remembers the people, places, and events of those times that continue to have an impact on his life and his identity today. The author explores several key themes in the process, and he invites readers to think about their own life journeys and faith stories at the same time.

Chapter 1

Winter of Wonder, Spring of Promise

In chapter 1, the author reflects on what his world was like when he was a boy of ten; and he talks about the simple joys and struggles of living then, including his early memories of faith, family, and the Bible.

1. Why do people often talk about and reflect upon the world in which they grew up? What can be gained by looking back at our past?

2. Discuss the importance of the tenth year in a child's life. For example, how does a ten-year-old view the world, and what are some of the influences that shape a person at that age? Share a memory of your tenth year of life.

3. Why does the world often seem simpler in the past? List some of the pros and cons of life decades ago as compared with today. (Try to separate fact from fiction.)

4. What role do you believe imagination played in the author's boyhood world? Is imagination as important today as it was then? Discuss.

5. What are some ways in which people use the Bible to suit their own purposes, either intentionally or unintentionally?

6. What do you admire about the "Greatest Generation"—the generation of the Great Depression and World War II? Discuss the manner in which they lived, and the role their faith has played.

7. What memories did reading this chapter stir up for you? Connect your memories and relate them to your faith journey.

8. What additional insights or questions from this chapter would you like to explore?

Chapter 2

Born Again

In chapter 2, the author talks about his altar-call conversion experience, and he examines what it means to be "born again."

1. Who or what influenced your faith as a child? Share an early memory of church or of your thoughts about God.

2. What religious beliefs and traditions did you see as the norm while growing up? Did you know people of other faith traditions; and if so, how did you view them?

3. In your own words, what does it mean to be "born again"? What sort of changes does a new life in Christ bring?

4. Why might some people feel uncomfortable with the idea of "being saved," or with that terminology? Are "being saved" and "being born again" simply two different ways to talk about the same thing? Explain.

5. Can you name a date or a time when you made a personal commitment to Christ? Share your spiritual turning point.

6. Does a conversion experience have to be dramatic in order to be effective? Why or why not?

7. Talk about the meaning behind the author's statement that it isn't enough to be born again; one also needs to grow up. How can we guard against self-righteousness?

8. What additional insights or questions from this chapter would you like to explore?

Chapter 3

A Call Is for Those Who Hear It

Chapter 3 looks at the concept of a call to ministry as a Christian, and how events and other people may influence that call.

1. Discuss what it means to feel "called." How does a call differ from person to person?

2. Identify and list human elements and factors that enter into the process of a calling to any career or personal vocation.

3. Explain the meaning behind the title of this chapter, "A Call Is for Those Who Hear It."

4. The author briefly mentions how some people may feel strongly called to a particular mission, while in truth they are better suited for something else. Talk about possible reasons why this happens, and how you might respond to a friend or family member whom you felt was missing his or her true calling.

5. How did your family and friends help or hinder your spiritual growth or your sense of being called?

6. What insights into how a ministry for Christ begins, and how a faith grows, did you receive from reading this chapter?

7. What are some ways we as a faith community can be more helpful to young people as they seek to discern their life's call, including those who are thinking about entering into professional ministry?

8. What additional insights or questions from this chapter would you like to explore?

Chapter 4

Benito Mussolini and the Blue Eagle

In chapter 4 the author talks about national and world circumstances that shaped Depression-era views on the end times, and he stresses the usefulness of living life with a sense of urgency.

1. What national program does the author say the Blue Eagle represented? What symbols or slogans of national pride do you recall from your childhood years?

2. According to the author, what sort of fears did people have about Mussolini and about a symbol such as the Blue Eagle?

3. What were some of the circumstances in the Depression era that encouraged apocalyptic preaching and the belief that the end times were near?

4. Discuss how hard times, including economic uncertainty, affect a person's faith.

5. Do you personally spend much time thinking about the end times and the return of Jesus Christ? Why or why not? How do circumstances and events in our world today influence your thinking in that regard?

6. What did the author mean by the statement, "Only the rarest of saints in the rarest of moments wants God for God's sake alone"? What does that suggest about our motives for anticipating Christ's return?

7. In what ways is a sense of urgency valuable?

8. What additional insights or questions from this chapter would you like to explore?

Chapter 5

I'm a Child of the King

Chapter 5 examines the ways people coped with poverty during the 1930s and how faith helped them survive.

1. Share some of the factors that have most influenced your life. What dreams or goals did you aspire to as a child?

2. Share some memories about your grade-school education. Do you feel that you received a quality education? What factors helped or hindered you?

3. Discuss the conditions and the pains of poverty. Do you agree with the author that the worst pain associated with poverty is feeling "different"? Explain.

4. Do you see poverty as a prevalent problem today? Why or why not? How important is money to having a good quality of life?

5. Talk about the concept of "making do with what you've got." Is this something we know much about today? Why or why not?

6. What examples of faith, hope, and perseverance are found in this chapter? How does faith in God help people through tough times?

7. In your own words, what does it mean to be a child of the King? When has your personal relationship with Christ "pulled you through" tough times?

8. What additional insights or questions from this chapter would you like to explore?

Chapter 6

From Every Dime, a Penny

In chapter 6 the author further discusses financial hardships during the Great Depression, and he shows why tithing should be considered a lasting investment.

1. Share a memory of someone, perhaps a non-family member, who invested in you as a child.

2. What schoolteacher or Sunday-school teacher made a lasting impression on you? Explain. How did you learn about what it means to be generous?

3. Share something about your personal experience (or lack thereof) with making and following a budget. What are the challenges? What tips or advice can you offer?

4. What lessons about tithing can be found in this chapter?

5. In what ways is tithing a "lifetime investment program," and an investment in people?

6. Are there "correct" or "incorrect" motivations for giving? Explain.

7. Besides tithing, what are some additional ways you can invest in others?

8. What additional insights or questions from this chapter would you like to explore?

Chapter 7

How Can You Be a Preacher
If You Haven't Read the Bible Through?

Chapter 7 shows the benefits of reading and rereading the Bible over a lifetime.

1. What impact did the Reverend Gene Palmer have on the life of the author?

2. What person, or what circumstances, have encouraged you to read the Bible? Share some details about your practice or habits of reading the Bible.

3. What is it about the Bible that interests or enriches you most? If possible, share some of your favorite books or passages from the Bible, and explain why you like them.

4. What are the benefits of reading the Bible through from beginning to end?

5. What did the author mean by his comment that the Bible is a very "uneven" book?

6. What are the benefits of reading the Bible again and again, even after you have read the entire Bible through?

7. Discuss ways you can challenge and encourage both yourself and others to read the Bible.

8. What additional insights or questions from this chapter would you like to explore?

Chapter 8

Promises Are for Believers

Chapter 8 examines the promises of God as found in the Bible, who those promises are meant for, and what they represent.

1. Name and discuss some of God's promises that are found in the Bible.

2. Share a time when one of God's promises took on great importance for you.

3. Describe what the author meant by his particular use of the term *believer.* What are your own thoughts on what it means to be a believer?

4. What role does sin play in our faith? What role does doubt play?

5. What lessons can we learn from the biblical story of Jesus being tempted by Satan?

6. Explain what the author meant when he wrote, "The greatest promise is God."

7. What additional insights or questions from this chapter would you like to explore?

8. If you have not already done so, take a few moments now to read the author's concluding remarks in "A Summing Up." Then take a few moments to reflect again upon your own life and to connect your memories to your faith story. How has the time you have spent with this book enriched you and strengthened your Christian faith?